AI Crash C

Build Your First Artificial Intelligence Projects Step-by-Step

BOOKER BLUNT

All rights reserved

Table of Content

TABLE OF CONTENTS

3

INTRODUCTION

Artificial Intelligence (AI) is no longer a futuristic concept—it's here, shaping industries, revolutionizing how we interact with technology, and transforming our daily lives. From healthcare diagnostics to autonomous driving, AI is embedded in the systems we rely on every day. However, with such vast potential comes a growing need for understanding, building, and responsibly deploying AI systems. This book is designed to be your comprehensive guide to understanding and building AI applications, from the ground up, using practical, hands-on techniques and real-world examples.

This book, **"AI Crash Course: Build Your First Artificial Intelligence Projects Step-by-Step"**, is aimed at both beginners and those with some experience in machine learning, looking to enhance their knowledge and skills in AI. Whether you're a software developer, data scientist, or enthusiast eager to dive into AI, this book will equip you with the knowledge and tools necessary to create impactful AI projects.

Why This Book?

AI is one of the most transformative technologies of our time. It powers everything from virtual assistants like Siri and Alexa to self-driving cars and predictive health models. However, as exciting as AI is, it can also be daunting to navigate, given the sheer volume of techniques, algorithms, and tools available. This book simplifies that journey by providing a **step-by-step approach** to building AI applications, with a focus on hands-on learning.

Throughout the chapters, you will:

- **Understand Core AI Concepts**: We start with the basics of AI, including its history, its impact on various industries, and the technologies that power it.
- **Learn the Tools of the Trade**: Python, the most widely used programming language for AI development, serves as the foundation. We dive deep into the key libraries, such as **NumPy**, **Pandas**, **TensorFlow**, **Keras**, and more, giving you the tools to handle data, build models, and train your AI systems.
- **Work on Real-World Projects**: You will not only understand the theoretical aspects of AI but also

apply them through projects, including building a **personal assistant**, **chatbots**, and **recommendation systems**. These projects will help you develop the critical skills needed to tackle complex AI problems.

- **Explore Ethical AI**: As AI becomes more prevalent, it is essential to consider the ethical implications of building intelligent systems. This book introduces you to the ethical considerations in AI, including bias, transparency, and the impact of AI on society.

What You'll Build and Learn:

- **AI Personal Assistant**: This hands-on project teaches you to integrate multiple AI techniques, such as **speech recognition**, **NLP (Natural Language Processing)**, and task automation, into a fully functional assistant that can set reminders, fetch weather data, and manage a to-do list.
- **AI-Powered Chatbots**: You will create both **rule-based** and **AI-driven chatbots**, learning the basics of NLP and machine learning to develop intelligent agents capable of carrying on meaningful conversations.
- **Recommendation Systems**: Learn how to build systems like the ones used by Amazon, Netflix, and

Spotify to personalize recommendations for users based on their preferences and behaviors.

- **AI Debugging and Optimization**: Understand how to troubleshoot and optimize your models. Learn best practices for improving performance and avoiding common pitfalls like **overfitting** and **underfitting**.

Why AI Matters:

AI is everywhere: it's transforming healthcare, revolutionizing finance, optimizing marketing campaigns, and even driving social change. The rise of AI has led to the automation of tasks that once required human intervention, allowing businesses to operate more efficiently, make data-driven decisions, and create innovative products and services. However, with great power comes great responsibility.

This book not only teaches you to create AI models but also introduces you to the **ethical considerations** that come with using these powerful technologies. You will learn to build models that are transparent, accountable, and ethical, ensuring that your AI applications benefit everyone.

A Step-by-Step Approach to Learning AI:

The journey through this book is structured to take you from beginner to confident AI developer. Here's what you can expect:

- **Foundations of AI**: We start with the essentials: What is AI? What are machine learning and deep learning? How do they differ? What tools and libraries are commonly used in AI? You will learn the building blocks that form the foundation of all AI models.

- **Hands-On Projects**: In each chapter, you'll work on practical projects that put your knowledge to use. These projects are designed to build your confidence and provide tangible outcomes that showcase your skills.

- **Practical Techniques**: We focus on hands-on learning and practical techniques that you can directly apply to real-world problems. Whether it's using **scikit-learn** for machine learning models or **TensorFlow** for deep learning, you will gain practical experience in building AI systems.

- **Advanced Concepts**: As we progress, you will tackle more advanced topics like **neural networks**,

reinforcement learning, and **AI deployment** in production systems. The goal is to ensure you are well-prepared to create sophisticated AI applications.

Who Should Read This Book?

- **Beginners**: If you're just getting started with AI and machine learning, this book provides an accessible introduction with clear explanations, examples, and hands-on projects.
- **Developers**: If you're a software developer with basic knowledge of programming and want to add AI to your skill set, this book will help you get started quickly and effectively.
- **Data Scientists**: If you're already familiar with machine learning and want to expand your knowledge to deep learning, NLP, and AI application development, this book will deepen your understanding and provide the tools needed to work on real-world AI projects.

11

What You Will Take Away From This Book:

By the end of this book, you will have the confidence to develop AI-powered applications, build machine learning models, and deploy them in real-world environments. You will have the skills to create personalized, intelligent systems that can process data, learn from experience, and make decisions—skills that are highly sought after in today's data-driven world.

Final Thoughts:

AI is transforming the world, and the need for skilled AI practitioners is greater than ever. This book provides a hands-on, practical approach to learning AI and equipping you with the tools you need to succeed in this exciting field. Whether you're looking to build an AI personal assistant, develop intelligent recommendation systems, or dive into complex deep learning models, this book will be your roadmap.

Let's get started and unlock the world of artificial intelligence together!

CHAPTER 1

INTRODUCTION TO ARTIFICIAL INTELLIGENCE

Artificial Intelligence (AI) is no longer a futuristic concept; it is an integral part of our daily lives, from the way we interact with our devices to the way businesses make decisions. This chapter will provide a broad overview of AI, its applications, and its societal impact. We will also explore the distinctions between AI, Machine Learning (ML), and Deep Learning (DL), and discuss why learning AI is becoming increasingly important. Additionally, we will look at real-world examples of how AI is transforming industries like healthcare, finance, and entertainment.

1.1 What is AI?

Artificial Intelligence (AI) refers to the ability of a machine or computer system to perform tasks that typically require human intelligence. These tasks can include problem-solving, decision-making, understanding natural language, recognizing patterns, and even mimicking human behavior. AI systems can process vast amounts of data, make predictions, and improve over time through learning and experience.

In simple terms, AI enables machines to "think" and act autonomously, simulating human-like cognitive functions.

Key Types of AI:

- **Narrow AI (Weak AI)**: Designed for a specific task, such as facial recognition, recommendation systems, or self-driving cars.
- **General AI (Strong AI)**: Hypothetical AI that possesses the ability to perform any intellectual task that a human being can do. This type of AI does not yet exist.

AI is powered by algorithms, statistical models, and large datasets, allowing it to learn patterns and make decisions that improve with time and data input.

Applications of AI:

AI has broad applications across various sectors. Some common areas where AI is already being used include:

- **Natural Language Processing (NLP)**: AI enables machines to understand and interpret human language. Voice assistants like Siri, Alexa, and Google Assistant rely on NLP to process speech and provide useful responses.
- **Computer Vision**: AI allows machines to interpret and make decisions based on visual input. For example, self-driving cars use computer vision to navigate and detect obstacles.
- **Predictive Analytics**: AI models can predict future outcomes based on historical data, such as predicting stock market trends or consumer behavior.

1.2 The Difference Between AI, Machine Learning, and Deep Learning

While these terms are often used interchangeably, they represent different concepts, each with its own scope and capabilities. Understanding these distinctions will give you a clearer picture of the AI landscape.

Artificial Intelligence (AI):

AI is the overarching field that encompasses all techniques that enable computers to simulate human intelligence. AI can be rule-based (using predefined rules) or data-driven (learning from data), and it includes a wide range of techniques, from simple algorithms to more complex models.

Machine Learning (ML):

Machine Learning is a subset of AI focused on building systems that learn from data. Unlike traditional AI, which follows explicit instructions, ML allows systems to learn from examples and make predictions without being explicitly programmed.

- **Supervised Learning**: The algorithm learns from labeled data (e.g., classifying emails as spam or not).
- **Unsupervised Learning**: The system finds hidden patterns in data without labeled examples (e.g., clustering customers based on behavior).

- **Reinforcement Learning**: The model learns by interacting with an environment and receiving feedback (e.g., training an agent to play a game).

Deep Learning (DL):

Deep Learning is a specialized subset of Machine Learning that uses neural networks with many layers (hence the term "deep"). These networks are inspired by the human brain and can automatically learn to represent data in increasingly abstract ways. Deep learning has been behind many breakthroughs in AI, particularly in areas like image recognition and natural language understanding.

- **Convolutional Neural Networks (CNNs)** are often used for image processing.
- **Recurrent Neural Networks (RNNs)** are used for sequence data, such as speech and text.

In summary:

- **AI** is the broad concept of machines performing tasks that require human-like intelligence.
- **ML** is a subset of AI that focuses on systems that can learn from data.

- **DL** is a subset of ML that uses deep neural networks to process large amounts of data and extract high-level features.

1.3 Why Learn AI?

AI is revolutionizing every industry and shaping the future of technology. Here are some key reasons why learning AI is becoming more essential:

1. High Demand for AI Skills:

AI is one of the fastest-growing fields in technology. According to various industry reports, the demand for AI professionals has surged over the last few years, with companies in almost every sector seeking talent to help them adopt AI and machine learning solutions. By learning AI, you position yourself for roles in diverse industries, including technology, healthcare, finance, and manufacturing.

2. AI's Impact on Industries:

AI is not just a buzzword; it is actively reshaping business operations and creating new opportunities. From automating repetitive tasks to making complex decisions based on large data sets, AI improves efficiency and drives innovation.

3. Competitive Advantage:

Businesses that leverage AI to streamline operations, enhance customer experience, or develop innovative products gain a significant edge over competitors. As AI technology becomes more accessible, it is important for individuals and organizations to stay ahead of the curve.

4. Expanding Career Opportunities:

AI-related job roles, such as AI engineer, data scientist, machine learning researcher, and AI consultant, are on the rise. These roles not only offer lucrative salaries but also provide the opportunity to work on cutting-edge projects that shape the future of technology.

5. AI for Problem Solving:

AI has the potential to solve complex global challenges. From climate change predictions to personalized medicine, AI can be applied to address some of the world's most pressing problems. Learning AI allows you to contribute to innovations that improve the world.

6. Innovation in Everyday Life:

AI is already integrated into our daily lives through devices like smartphones, home assistants, and recommendation systems. As AI continues to evolve, its integration into applications like autonomous vehicles, healthcare diagnostics, and personalized learning will continue to grow, affecting both individual lives and the economy.

1.4 Real-World Examples of AI

AI is already being used in a wide variety of industries. Let's take a closer look at how AI is being implemented in real-world applications:

1. Healthcare:

AI is transforming the healthcare industry by improving diagnostic accuracy, enhancing treatment options, and streamlining administrative tasks.

- **Medical Imaging**: AI algorithms can analyze medical images, such as X-rays, MRIs, and CT scans, to detect conditions like tumors or fractures with high accuracy.

- **Personalized Medicine**: Machine learning models predict the most effective treatment based on a patient's unique genetic makeup and medical history.
- **Drug Discovery**: AI systems can analyze molecular data to discover potential new drugs, speeding up the process of bringing new treatments to market.

2. Finance:

In the finance industry, AI is used for everything from fraud detection to algorithmic trading.

- **Fraud Detection**: Machine learning models analyze transaction patterns to detect suspicious activity, helping financial institutions prevent fraud.
- **Algorithmic Trading**: AI systems make split-second decisions on stock market investments, analyzing vast amounts of data and predicting market movements.
- **Customer Service**: AI-powered chatbots and virtual assistants are used to manage customer queries, allowing businesses to provide 24/7 support.

3. Entertainment:

AI is reshaping how we consume entertainment, from personalized recommendations to content creation.

- **Recommendation Systems**: Platforms like Netflix, Spotify, and YouTube use AI to recommend movies, music, and videos based on your preferences and past behavior.
- **Content Creation**: AI is being used to generate music, art, and even scripts for TV shows and movies. This helps creators produce content more efficiently.
- **Gaming**: AI-driven characters in video games provide more dynamic and engaging experiences, learning from player behavior to adapt and challenge the player.

4. Retail:

AI is enhancing the customer experience and driving operational efficiency in retail.

- **Personalized Shopping**: E-commerce platforms like Amazon use AI to recommend products based on your shopping history, preferences, and browsing behavior.

- **Inventory Management**: AI is used to predict demand for products, optimizing stock levels and reducing waste.
- **Chatbots for Customer Service**: Many retail businesses use AI-powered chatbots to provide instant customer support and resolve common queries.

5. Autonomous Vehicles:

AI is at the heart of self-driving technology, enabling vehicles to navigate safely without human intervention.

- **Self-Driving Cars**: Companies like Tesla and Waymo are using AI algorithms to enable vehicles to drive autonomously, making decisions based on real-time data from sensors and cameras.
- **Traffic Management**: AI systems can optimize traffic flow in cities, reducing congestion and improving overall efficiency.

6. Smart Cities:

AI is being used to enhance urban life by improving infrastructure, energy management, and public safety.

- **Energy Efficiency**: AI optimizes the use of energy in smart buildings and grids, reducing energy consumption and lowering costs.
- **Traffic Monitoring**: AI analyzes traffic patterns to optimize traffic lights and reduce congestion in cities.
- **Public Safety**: AI-powered surveillance systems monitor public areas for potential security threats, enhancing the safety of citizens.

Summary

In this chapter, we:

- Gained a broad overview of **Artificial Intelligence**, its **applications**, and its **impact on society**.
- Explored the **difference between AI, Machine Learning, and Deep Learning**, understanding the distinctions and how they relate.

- Discussed **why learning AI** is crucial for future career growth, its demand in the job market, and its transformative power across industries.
- Examined **real-world examples** of AI, including its use in healthcare, finance, entertainment, retail, autonomous vehicles, and smart cities.

AI is not just a field of study but a rapidly evolving force that is shaping our future. As we progress through the book, we will dive deeper into how to build AI models and projects step-by-step, providing you with the skills to not only understand AI but also to create your own AI-powered solutions.

CHAPTER 2

GETTING STARTED WITH

PYTHON FOR AI

Python has emerged as the go-to language for **Artificial Intelligence (AI)** and **data science** because of its simplicity, versatility, and a rich ecosystem of libraries. In this chapter, we'll explore why Python is the preferred language for AI development, how to set up a Python environment, and introduce the key libraries you will use when building AI projects. We will also cover basic Python concepts that are essential for working with AI, such as data types, loops, and functions.

2.1 Why Python? Why Python is the Most Popular Language for AI and Data Science

Python has become the **de facto standard** for AI development for a variety of reasons:

1. Simple and Readable Syntax

Python is known for its **simple, easy-to-read syntax**, making it a great choice for both beginners and experienced developers. The code is intuitive and closely mirrors natural language, which allows you to focus on solving problems rather than getting bogged down by complex syntax.

2. Extensive Libraries and Frameworks

Python boasts an extensive collection of libraries and frameworks designed specifically for AI, machine learning, and data science. Some popular libraries include:

- **NumPy**: For numerical computations and handling arrays.
- **Pandas**: For data manipulation and analysis.
- **Matplotlib**: For creating data visualizations.
- **Scikit-learn**: For machine learning algorithms and tools.
- **TensorFlow** and **PyTorch**: For deep learning models.
- **Keras**: For building neural networks with ease.
- **NLTK** and **spaCy**: For natural language processing (NLP).

These libraries simplify the development process, allowing you to build powerful AI models without needing to reinvent the wheel.

3. Community Support

Python has a **large and active community** of developers, researchers, and practitioners in the AI field. This makes it easy to find resources, documentation, tutorials, and support from others working on similar problems. Additionally, many AI researchers and companies publish their code in Python, further contributing to its growth and popularity.

4. Versatility and Flexibility

Python is **versatile**, allowing you to use it for a wide range of applications beyond AI, such as web development, automation, and data analysis. This versatility makes Python a one-stop solution for building end-to-end AI systems that integrate with other parts of a software stack.

5. Integration Capabilities

Python is well-suited for integrating with other technologies and platforms. It can interact with various databases, web frameworks, and APIs, making it an excellent choice for AI projects that need to operate in a larger tech ecosystem.

Because of these advantages, Python has become the **language of choice** for AI and data science, empowering developers to create sophisticated AI systems quickly and efficiently.

2.2 Setting Up Python: Installing Python and Setting Up a Development Environment

Before diving into AI projects, you need to set up your Python development environment. Here's a step-by-step guide to installing Python and preparing the environment for AI development:

1. Installing Python

Python can be installed easily on various operating systems.

- **Windows**:
    - Go to the official Python website: https://www.python.org/downloads/
    - Download the latest stable version (Python 3.x).

29

- During installation, ensure that the **"Add Python to PATH"** checkbox is selected.

- To verify the installation, open a command prompt and type:

```bash

python --version
```

- **MacOS**:

  - Python is usually pre-installed on macOS, but you may want to install a newer version.

  - Install Python using **Homebrew**:

```bash

brew install python
```

- **Linux**:

  - On most Linux distributions, Python comes pre-installed. However, you can update to the latest version with:

```bash

sudo apt-get update
sudo apt-get install python3
```

2. Installing a Code Editor or IDE

Choose a development environment that suits you:

- **VS Code**: A powerful, lightweight code editor with many plugins for Python and AI development.
- **PyCharm**: A popular IDE specifically designed for Python, with built-in tools for managing projects and debugging.
- **Jupyter Notebooks**: Ideal for data science and AI development, as it allows you to run Python code interactively in cells.

To install **VS Code** or **PyCharm**, simply download and install from their respective websites. If you're using **Jupyter Notebooks**, you can install it by running:

```bash

pip install notebook
```

3. Setting Up a Virtual Environment

A **virtual environment** allows you to manage dependencies separately for each project, ensuring that they don't interfere with each other. This is especially important when working with different versions of libraries.

31

To create a virtual environment, use the following steps:

1. Create a project folder.
2. Inside the folder, create a virtual environment:

```bash

python -m venv myenv
```

3. Activate the virtual environment:
   o **Windows**:

```bash

myenv\Scripts\activate
```

   o **MacOS/Linux**:

```bash

source myenv/bin/activate
```

Once activated, any packages you install will be confined to this environment, avoiding potential version conflicts.

4. Installing Required Libraries

For AI development, we need several key libraries:

```bash
bash
```

```
pip install numpy pandas matplotlib scikit-learn
tensorflow keras
```

These libraries will enable you to work with numerical data, perform machine learning tasks, visualize data, and build AI models.

2.3 Using Python Libraries: An Introduction to Key Libraries

To build AI models, we need to become familiar with a few essential Python libraries. Below is an introduction to some of the most widely used libraries in AI development:

1. NumPy: Numerical Computing and Array Handling

NumPy is the core library for numerical computing in Python. It provides support for handling large, multi-dimensional arrays and matrices, along with a collection of mathematical functions to operate on these arrays.

Example:

```python
python
```

```
import numpy as np

# Create a 2D array
arr = np.array([[1, 2], [3, 4]])

# Perform element-wise addition
arr_sum = arr + 5
print(arr_sum)
```

2. Pandas: Data Manipulation and Analysis

Pandas is an essential library for data manipulation and analysis, particularly for working with tabular data. It provides two primary data structures: `Series` (1D) and `DataFrame` (2D), which allow for easy manipulation of datasets.

Example:

```python
python

import pandas as pd

# Load a dataset into a DataFrame
df = pd.read_csv("data.csv")

# Display the first few rows
print(df.head())
```

```
# Filter rows based on conditions
filtered_data = df[df['age'] > 30]
```

3. Matplotlib: Data Visualization

Matplotlib is the go-to library for visualizing data in Python. It allows you to create various types of plots and charts, such as line plots, bar charts, and histograms.

Example:

```
python
```

```
import matplotlib.pyplot as plt

# Plot a simple line graph
x = [1, 2, 3, 4, 5]
y = [1, 4, 9, 16, 25]

plt.plot(x, y)
plt.xlabel('X-axis')
plt.ylabel('Y-axis')
plt.title('Simple Line Plot')
plt.show()
```

4. Scikit-learn: Machine Learning

Scikit-learn is a powerful machine learning library that provides simple and efficient tools for data mining and data analysis. It supports a variety of algorithms for classification, regression, clustering, and dimensionality reduction.

Example:

```python
from sklearn.ensemble import RandomForestClassifier
from sklearn.datasets import load_iris
from sklearn.model_selection import train_test_split

# Load the Iris dataset
data = load_iris()
X = data.data
y = data.target

# Split data into training and testing sets
X_train, X_test, y_train, y_test = train_test_split(X, y, test_size=0.2)

# Train a RandomForest model
model = RandomForestClassifier()
model.fit(X_train, y_train)

# Predict on the test set
predictions = model.predict(X_test)
print(predictions)
```

5. TensorFlow and Keras: Deep Learning

TensorFlow is an open-source library developed by Google for deep learning. Keras is an API built on top of TensorFlow that simplifies the process of building neural networks.

Example using **Keras**:

python

```
from keras.models import Sequential
from keras.layers import Dense

# Build a simple neural network
model = Sequential([
    Dense(32, activation='relu', input_dim=64),
    Dense(10, activation='softmax')
])

# Compile the model
model.compile(optimizer='adam',
loss='categorical_crossentropy',
metrics=['accuracy'])

# Train the model
model.fit(X_train,      y_train,      epochs=10,
batch_size=32)
```

2.4 Basic Python Concepts for AI

While Python is known for its simplicity, understanding the basic programming concepts is essential for building AI systems. Here are some key Python concepts that are frequently used in AI:

1. Data Types

Python has several built-in data types such as integers, floats, strings, lists, tuples, and dictionaries. In AI, you will often work with numerical data, lists, and arrays.

Example:

```python

# Integer
age = 25

# Float
height = 5.8

# String
name = "John Doe"

# List (used for storing multiple items)
numbers = [1, 2, 3, 4, 5]
```

2. Loops

Loops are used to repeat a block of code multiple times. In AI, loops are often used to iterate over datasets or repeatedly train machine learning models.

Example:

```python
# Looping through a list of numbers
for number in numbers:
    print(number)

# While loop (runs until the condition is False)
count = 0
while count < 5:
    print(count)
    count += 1
```

3. Functions

Functions allow you to group code into reusable blocks. In AI, you'll create functions to handle tasks like data preprocessing or model evaluation.

Example:

```python
```

```
# Function to calculate the square of a number
def square(num):
    return num ** 2

result = square(5)
print(result)
```

Summary

In this chapter, we:

- Explored **why Python** is the go-to language for AI, highlighting its simplicity, powerful libraries, and community support.
- Walked through the steps to **set up Python**, including installing Python, setting up a virtual environment, and installing key libraries like NumPy, Pandas, Matplotlib, and Scikit-learn.
- Introduced fundamental Python concepts like **data types**, **loops**, and **functions**, which are essential for building AI models and working with data.
- Gained a basic understanding of how to use Python libraries for AI tasks, such as data manipulation, visualization, and machine learning.

With this solid foundation in Python, you're ready to dive into the world of AI. In the next chapter, we will cover **machine learning basics**, including key algorithms and how to build your first machine learning model.

CHAPTER 3

UNDERSTANDING MACHINE LEARNING BASICS

Machine Learning (ML) is one of the most powerful tools in Artificial Intelligence, enabling systems to learn and make decisions from data without being explicitly programmed. In this chapter, we will explore the fundamentals of machine learning, including key concepts like **supervised** vs **unsupervised learning**, an introduction to some basic machine learning algorithms, and how to build your first machine learning model using **Scikit-learn**, one of the most widely used machine learning libraries in Python.

3.1 What is Machine Learning?

Machine Learning (ML) is a subset of **Artificial Intelligence (AI)** that enables machines to learn patterns from data and make predictions or decisions based on those patterns. Instead of being explicitly programmed to perform

42

specific tasks, a machine learning model improves its performance on tasks by learning from data over time.

There are three primary types of machine learning:

- **Supervised Learning**
- **Unsupervised Learning**
- **Reinforcement Learning**

1. Supervised Learning

In **supervised learning**, the model is trained on a labeled dataset, meaning that each data point has a corresponding target value (label). The goal is for the model to learn the relationship between the input features (X) and the output labels (Y), so it can predict the output for new, unseen data.

Common supervised learning tasks include:

- **Classification**: Predicting a category or label for a given input. For example, identifying whether an email is spam or not.
- **Regression**: Predicting a continuous value. For example, predicting house prices based on various features like square footage and location.

2. Unsupervised Learning

In **unsupervised learning**, the model is trained on data without labeled outputs. The goal is to find patterns or structure within the data. It's commonly used for clustering data into groups or reducing the dimensionality of data.

Common unsupervised learning tasks include:

- **Clustering**: Grouping similar data points together. For example, segmenting customers based on their purchasing behavior.
- **Dimensionality Reduction**: Reducing the number of features in a dataset while maintaining its structure. An example of this is Principal Component Analysis (PCA).

3. Reinforcement Learning

Reinforcement learning is a type of machine learning where an agent learns by interacting with its environment and receiving feedback in the form of rewards or penalties. This method is often used in gaming, robotics, and autonomous systems.

3.2 Key Algorithms

Machine learning models rely on various algorithms to learn from data. Let's explore some of the most commonly used algorithms for both **supervised** and **unsupervised** learning.

1. Linear Regression (Supervised Learning)

Linear regression is one of the simplest and most widely used algorithms in machine learning. It is used for **regression tasks** and predicts a continuous value based on the linear relationship between input features and the target variable.

Formula: The linear regression model fits the best line (line of best fit) to the data. The equation is:

$y=mx+by = mx + by=mx+b$

Where:

- yyy is the predicted value.
- mmm is the slope of the line.
- xxx is the input feature.
- bbb is the y-intercept.

2. Decision Trees (Supervised Learning)

A decision tree is a flowchart-like structure where each internal node represents a decision based on a feature, and each leaf node represents a class label (in classification) or a continuous value (in regression).

The decision tree works by splitting the data at each node based on a feature that results in the most informative partitions, using metrics like **Gini impurity** or **entropy** for classification.

3. K-Nearest Neighbors (KNN) (Supervised Learning)

K-Nearest Neighbors (KNN) is a simple and intuitive classification algorithm. It works by finding the K nearest data points to a new sample and assigning the most common class among those neighbors to the new data point.

For example, if you want to classify a fruit based on its color and size, KNN would classify it by looking at the closest data points (fruits with similar features) and determining the majority class.

- **K** is a user-defined parameter that controls how many neighbors should be considered.

4. K-Means Clustering (Unsupervised Learning)

K-Means is one of the most popular clustering algorithms. It works by partitioning data into KKK clusters, where each cluster has a centroid (mean value of all points within that cluster). The algorithm assigns each data point to the nearest centroid and updates the centroids iteratively.

3.3 Training and Testing Data

One of the most important steps in machine learning is **splitting the dataset** into training and testing sets. This ensures that the model is not overfitting and that it can generalize well to new, unseen data.

1. Training Data:

Training data is used to teach the model. During the training process, the model learns the patterns and relationships within the data to make predictions or classifications. The more data you provide, the better the model can learn from it.

2. Testing Data:

The testing data is used to evaluate the model's performance after it has been trained. The testing data should not be used during training to prevent overfitting, where the model becomes too tailored to the training data and performs poorly on new data.

3. Train-Test Split:

A common practice is to split the data into two sets: a **training set** (usually 80% of the data) and a **testing set** (usually 20% of the data). This ensures that the model is evaluated on data it has never seen before, providing a more accurate measure of its performance.

```python
from sklearn.model_selection import train_test_split
X = data.drop('target', axis=1)  # Input features
y = data['target']  # Target variable

X_train, X_test, y_train, y_test = train_test_split(X, y, test_size=0.2, random_state=42)
```

In this code:

- x represents the input features, and y represents the target variable.
- The `train_test_split()` function splits the data into training and testing sets.

3.4 Building Your First Machine Learning Model: A Step-by-Step Walkthrough

Let's walk through building a simple **classification model** using the **K-Nearest Neighbors (KNN)** algorithm. In this example, we'll use the **Iris dataset**, a popular dataset in machine learning that contains measurements of different iris flowers and their species (setosa, versicolor, and virginica).

1. Importing Libraries

We'll start by importing the necessary libraries:

```python
import numpy as np
import pandas as pd
from sklearn.model_selection import train_test_split
```

```
from          sklearn.neighbors          import
KNeighborsClassifier
from sklearn.metrics import accuracy_score
from sklearn.datasets import load_iris
```

2. Loading the Data

We load the Iris dataset using **Scikit-learn**'s built-in `load_iris()` function.

python

```
# Load the Iris dataset
iris = load_iris()
X = iris.data   # Input features
y = iris.target  # Target variable (species)
```

3. Splitting the Data

We split the dataset into training and testing sets:

python

```
# Split the data into training and testing sets
X_train,    X_test,    y_train,    y_test    =
train_test_split(X,    y,    test_size=0.3,
random_state=42)
```

4. Creating the KNN Model

We create the **KNN classifier** and fit it to the training data:

50

```
python
```

```
# Create the KNN classifier
knn = KNeighborsClassifier(n_neighbors=3)
```

```
# Train the model
knn.fit(X_train, y_train)
```

5. Making Predictions

Once the model is trained, we can make predictions on the testing set:

```
python
```

```
# Make predictions on the test set
y_pred = knn.predict(X_test)
```

6. Evaluating the Model

Finally, we evaluate the model by calculating the **accuracy**:

```
python
```

```
# Evaluate the model's accuracy
accuracy = accuracy_score(y_test, y_pred)
print(f'Accuracy: {accuracy * 100:.2f}%')
```

In this example, we used the **K-Nearest Neighbors** algorithm to classify flower species based on their physical measurements. The model learned from the training data and made predictions on the testing data. The accuracy score tells us how well the model performed.

Summary

In this chapter, we:

- Gained an understanding of **Machine Learning (ML)** and the differences between **supervised**, **unsupervised**, and **reinforcement learning**.
- Learned about key machine learning algorithms such as **linear regression, decision trees**, and **KNN**.
- Understood the importance of **training** and **testing** data, and how to properly split datasets to avoid overfitting.
- Walked through building a **KNN classification model** using the Iris dataset, including model training, prediction, and evaluation.

With this foundation in machine learning basics, you are ready to dive deeper into more advanced techniques and applications. In the next chapter, we will explore **unsupervised learning** and work with clustering algorithms like **K-Means**.

CHAPTER 4

INTRODUCTION TO DATA PROCESSING AND CLEANING

Data is at the heart of Artificial Intelligence (AI) and Machine Learning (ML). Even the most sophisticated algorithms will fail if the data they are trained on is incomplete, inconsistent, or improperly formatted. Data processing and cleaning are crucial steps to ensure that machine learning models have access to high-quality, structured, and meaningful data. In this chapter, we will explore the importance of clean data, techniques for handling missing or corrupted data, how to create meaningful features, and the importance of data normalization and scaling. We will also walk through a real-world example of cleaning a dataset for a machine learning model.

4.1 Why Data Matters: The Importance of Clean and Organized Data for AI Models

The performance of an AI model depends heavily on the quality of the data it is trained on. **Garbage in, garbage out** is a common saying in data science, meaning that poor-quality data will lead to poor results, no matter how advanced the model is. Clean and organized data is essential for the following reasons:

1. Improving Accuracy and Performance

AI and machine learning models are built to **learn from data**, and they rely on that data to make predictions or decisions. If the data contains errors, outliers, or inconsistencies, the model may learn incorrect patterns, which can lead to inaccurate predictions and suboptimal performance.

2. Faster Convergence

When data is properly processed and cleaned, machine learning models tend to converge (i.e., reach optimal solutions) more quickly during training, leading to shorter training times and more efficient use of computational resources.

3. Avoiding Bias and Overfitting

Data issues, such as imbalanced or incomplete datasets, can cause **bias** in the model's predictions, affecting its ability to generalize well to new data. Proper data cleaning can help identify and mitigate these biases.

4. Enabling Feature Engineering

Clean data enables effective **feature engineering**, which involves creating new features from raw data that can better capture underlying patterns. Without clean data, it becomes difficult to engineer meaningful features that can improve the model's performance.

4.2 Handling Missing Data: Techniques to Handle Missing or Corrupted Data

Missing data is one of the most common issues in real-world datasets. Incomplete data can arise due to various reasons, such as errors in data collection, human mistakes, or simply due to missing information in surveys or records. Handling missing data is critical for building reliable machine learning models.

1. Identifying Missing Data

The first step in handling missing data is to identify where it occurs in your dataset. In Python, **Pandas** makes it easy to spot missing values using `isna()` or `isnull()` functions.

```python
import pandas as pd

# Example DataFrame with missing values
df = pd.DataFrame({
    'name': ['Alice', 'Bob', 'Charlie', None],
    'age': [25, 30, None, 35],
    'city': ['New York', None, 'Los Angeles', 'Chicago']
})

# Check for missing values
print(df.isna())
```

2. Removing Missing Data

If the missing data is minimal, you may choose to **drop** the rows or columns that contain missing values. This is typically done if the missing data doesn't carry enough significance to affect the analysis or model training.

```python
```

56

```
# Drop rows with any missing data
df_cleaned = df.dropna()
```

However, dropping data is usually not ideal, as you might lose valuable information. It's often better to **impute** missing values, especially if the missing data is large.

3. Imputing Missing Data

Imputation refers to filling in the missing values with a calculated or assumed value. Common strategies include:

- **Mean/Median/Mode Imputation**: Replace missing numerical values with the mean or median, and categorical values with the mode.
- **Predictive Imputation**: Use machine learning models to predict missing values based on the available data.

Example of **mean imputation**:

```
python
```

```
# Impute missing values in the 'age' column with
the mean
df['age'] = df['age'].fillna(df['age'].mean())
```

4. Advanced Imputation Techniques

For more complex scenarios, such as when there's a pattern to the missing data, machine learning algorithms like k-Nearest Neighbors (KNN) or regression models can be used to predict missing values.

4.3 Feature Engineering: Creating Meaningful Features from Raw Data

Feature engineering is the process of transforming raw data into meaningful features that can improve the performance of a machine learning model. Feature engineering often requires domain knowledge and creativity, as it involves identifying patterns in the data that the model can learn.

1. Creating New Features

- **Datetime Features**: For datasets with time-related data, you can create new features like the year, month, day, or weekday from a `datetime` column.

Example:

```
python
```

```
df['year'] = pd.to_datetime(df['date']).dt.year
df['month']                              =
pd.to_datetime(df['date']).dt.month
```

- **Categorical Variables**: Converting categorical variables into numerical form is essential for most machine learning models. You can use **one-hot encoding** or **label encoding** to convert categorical variables into numerical features.

python

```
# One-hot encoding for categorical column
df = pd.get_dummies(df, columns=['city'])
```

2. Handling Outliers

Outliers are extreme values that can skew the data and affect the model's performance. You can detect and handle outliers using methods like:

- **Z-score** or **IQR (Interquartile Range)** to identify outliers.
- **Capping or removing** outliers that fall outside a defined threshold.

python

59

```
# Remove outliers using IQR
Q1 = df['age'].quantile(0.25)
Q3 = df['age'].quantile(0.75)
IQR = Q3 - Q1
df = df[(df['age'] >= (Q1 - 1.5 * IQR)) &
(df['age'] <= (Q3 + 1.5 * IQR))]
```

3. Scaling and Normalization

Feature scaling is important for machine learning models, especially for algorithms that are sensitive to the scale of data (e.g., KNN, SVM, and neural networks). Standardizing the features to a consistent scale ensures the model treats all features equally.

4.4 Data Normalization and Scaling: Why It's Necessary and How to Do It

Data normalization and scaling are techniques used to standardize the range of independent variables or features of the data. These techniques are particularly important for algorithms that rely on distances between data points or the magnitude of features, such as **KNN, logistic regression,** and **neural networks**.

1. Why Normalize or Scale Data?

- **Distance-Based Models**: Algorithms like KNN and SVM rely on distance metrics, and if features are on different scales (e.g., age in years vs. income in thousands), it can affect the performance.

- **Convergence in Gradient-Based Optimization**: Models like **neural networks** and **logistic regression** use gradient descent for optimization. Features on very different scales can cause issues with convergence, leading to slow training times or poor performance.

2. Common Scaling Techniques

- **Min-Max Scaling**: Rescales the data to a fixed range, usually [0, 1].

```python
from sklearn.preprocessing import MinMaxScaler

scaler = MinMaxScaler()
df_scaled = scaler.fit_transform(df[['age',
'income']])
```

- **Standardization (Z-score normalization)**: Centers the data around 0 and scales it based on the standard deviation. This is often preferred for algorithms like linear regression and logistic regression.

```python

from sklearn.preprocessing import StandardScaler

scaler = StandardScaler()
df_standardized                                    =
scaler.fit_transform(df[['age', 'income']])
```

4.5 Real-World Example: Cleaning a Real Dataset for a Machine Learning Model

Now, let's walk through the process of cleaning a real-world dataset for use in a machine learning model. We'll use a **sample dataset** of customer information to build a model that predicts whether a customer will subscribe to a service (binary classification).

1. Loading the Dataset

We'll use the **Pandas** library to load and inspect the dataset.

```python
```

```
import pandas as pd

# Load the dataset
df = pd.read_csv("customer_data.csv")

# Display the first few rows of the dataset
print(df.head())
```

2. Handling Missing Data

We notice that some columns, such as age and income, have missing values. We'll impute missing values using the **mean** for numerical columns.

python

```
df['age'] = df['age'].fillna(df['age'].mean())
df['income']                                   =
df['income'].fillna(df['income'].mean())
```

3. Feature Engineering

We create a new feature, age_group, by categorizing customers into different age groups.

python

```
df['age_group'] = pd.cut(df['age'], bins=[0, 25,
45, 65, 100], labels=['Young', 'Middle-aged',
'Senior', 'Elderly'])
```

4. Encoding Categorical Variables

We need to convert categorical features into numerical form. For simplicity, let's use **one-hot encoding** for the age_group and subscription_type columns.

python

```
df = pd.get_dummies(df, columns=['age_group',
'subscription_type'])
```

5. Normalizing and Scaling Data

We scale the numerical features, such as age and income, using **standardization**.

python

```
from sklearn.preprocessing import StandardScaler

scaler = StandardScaler()
df[['age',            'income']]            =
scaler.fit_transform(df[['age', 'income']])
```

6. Splitting the Data

We split the data into training and testing sets.

```python
python

from          sklearn.model_selection          import
train_test_split

X = df.drop('subscription', axis=1)  # Features
y = df['subscription']  # Target variable

X_train,    X_test,    y_train,    y_test    =
train_test_split(X,    y,    test_size=0.2,
random_state=42)
```

Summary

In this chapter, we:

- Discussed the importance of clean, organized data for building effective AI models.
- Explored techniques to handle **missing data**, including imputation and removal.
- Learned about **feature engineering**, creating new meaningful features from raw data.
- Covered **data normalization and scaling** and why it is necessary for machine learning models.

- Walked through a **real-world example** of cleaning a dataset for use in a machine learning model, covering data preprocessing, feature creation, and scaling.

Data processing and cleaning is a crucial step in any machine learning pipeline. Clean, well-organized data allows machine learning models to perform optimally and accurately. In the next chapter, we will explore **supervised learning** in more detail, starting with algorithms like **linear regression** and **decision trees**.

CHAPTER 5

EXPLORING SUPERVISED

LEARNING

Supervised learning is one of the most widely used machine learning techniques. In supervised learning, the model is trained using labeled data, meaning that the input data comes with corresponding output labels or target values. The model learns to map inputs to outputs based on this labeled data and can then predict outcomes for new, unseen data. In this chapter, we will explore the concept of supervised learning, its two main types (regression and classification), and walk through how to build both types of models. Additionally, we will discuss the key performance metrics used to evaluate supervised learning models.

5.1 What is Supervised Learning?

Supervised learning is a type of machine learning where the algorithm learns from labeled training data. The main goal is for the model to learn a mapping function from inputs (features) to outputs (labels or target values) so that it can predict the output for new, unseen data.

Key Characteristics of Supervised Learning:

- **Labeled Data**: The dataset contains both input features and corresponding labels (or target values).
- **Training Process**: The algorithm uses this data to find patterns or relationships between inputs and outputs.
- **Prediction**: Once the model is trained, it can predict the output for new input data that it hasn't seen before.

Applications of Supervised Learning:

- **Predicting House Prices**: Based on features like square footage, number of bedrooms, and location.
- **Email Spam Detection**: Classifying emails as spam or not spam based on their content.
- **Medical Diagnosis**: Predicting whether a patient has a certain disease based on their medical history and test results.
- **Stock Price Prediction**: Forecasting the future stock price based on historical data.

Supervised learning is widely used in both **regression** tasks (predicting continuous values) and **classification** tasks (predicting categories or classes).

5.2 Regression vs Classification: The Difference Between Regression and Classification Tasks

In supervised learning, tasks can be broadly categorized into **regression** and **classification**. Both types of tasks involve predicting an outcome from input features, but the nature of the output (the target variable) differs.

1. Regression: Predicting Continuous Values

In regression tasks, the goal is to predict a continuous numeric value. The output (target) is a real number, such as predicting the price of a house or the temperature on a given day.

Example:

- Predicting house prices based on features like square footage, location, and number of bedrooms.
- Forecasting sales revenue for a business.

The most common algorithm for regression is **Linear Regression**.

2. Classification: Predicting Discrete Classes

In classification tasks, the goal is to predict a category or class label. The output is discrete, and the task involves assigning an input to one of several classes. For example, categorizing emails as **spam** or **not spam**.

Example:

- Predicting whether a customer will buy a product (Yes or No).
- Identifying whether an image contains a cat, dog, or bird.

Common algorithms for classification include **Decision Trees**, **Logistic Regression**, and **K-Nearest Neighbors (KNN)**.

5.3 Building a Regression Model: A Step-by-Step Guide to Building a Simple Linear Regression Model

Linear regression is a fundamental algorithm used in supervised learning for predicting continuous values. Let's go through the process of building a simple linear regression model using the **Scikit-learn** library in Python.

1. Importing Libraries and Dataset

First, let's import the necessary libraries and load a dataset. For this example, we'll use the **Boston housing dataset**, which contains features of houses (e.g., crime rate, average number of rooms) and the target variable (the price of the house).

python

```
import numpy as np
import pandas as pd
from sklearn.model_selection import train_test_split
from sklearn.linear_model import LinearRegression
from sklearn.metrics import mean_squared_error, r2_score
from sklearn.datasets import load_boston
```

```
# Load the dataset
data = load_boston()
X = data.data  # Features
y = data.target  # Target variable (house price)
```

2. Splitting the Data

Next, we split the data into training and testing sets. This ensures that we can train the model on one set of data and evaluate it on another.

python

```
X_train, X_test, y_train, y_test =
train_test_split(X, y, test_size=0.2,
random_state=42)
```

3. Creating the Linear Regression Model

Now, we create an instance of the **LinearRegression** class and fit the model to the training data.

python

```
# Create a linear regression model
model = LinearRegression()

# Train the model
model.fit(X_train, y_train)
```

4. Making Predictions

After training the model, we can use it to predict house prices for the test data.

python

```
# Make predictions on the test set
y_pred = model.predict(X_test)
```

5. Evaluating the Model

Finally, we evaluate the model's performance using metrics such as **Mean Squared Error (MSE)** and **R-squared (R^2)**. MSE measures the average squared difference between the predicted and actual values, while R^2 indicates how well the model explains the variance in the target variable.

python

```
# Calculate the Mean Squared Error (MSE)
mse = mean_squared_error(y_test, y_pred)
print(f"Mean Squared Error: {mse}")

# Calculate the R-squared value
r2 = r2_score(y_test, y_pred)
print(f"R-squared: {r2}")
```

5.4 Building a Classification Model: Creating a Classification Model with Decision Trees or Logistic Regression

Now, let's walk through building a **classification model** using **Decision Trees**, a widely used algorithm for classification tasks.

1. Importing Libraries and Dataset

Let's use the **Iris dataset**, which contains features of iris flowers (e.g., petal width, petal length) and the target variable (the species of the flower).

python

```python
from sklearn.datasets import load_iris
from sklearn.tree import DecisionTreeClassifier
from       sklearn.model_selection       import
train_test_split
from sklearn.metrics import accuracy_score

# Load the dataset
iris = load_iris()
X = iris.data  # Features
y = iris.target  # Target variable (species)
```

2. Splitting the Data

As with regression, we split the data into training and testing sets.

python

```
X_train,     X_test,     y_train,     y_test    =
train_test_split(X,        y,       test_size=0.2,
random_state=42)
```

3. Creating the Decision Tree Model

Now, we create an instance of the **DecisionTreeClassifier** class and fit the model to the training data.

python

```
# Create a decision tree classifier
model = DecisionTreeClassifier(random_state=42)

# Train the model
model.fit(X_train, y_train)
```

4. Making Predictions

Once the model is trained, we use it to predict the species of flowers in the test set.

python

```
# Make predictions on the test set
y_pred = model.predict(X_test)
```

5. Evaluating the Model

We evaluate the model's performance using **accuracy**, which is the percentage of correct predictions.

python

```
# Calculate the accuracy
accuracy = accuracy_score(y_test, y_pred)
print(f"Accuracy: {accuracy * 100:.2f}%")
```

5.5 Evaluating Models: Understanding Performance Metrics Like Accuracy, Precision, and Recall

Once we have built a machine learning model, it is crucial to assess its performance. Common evaluation metrics include:

1. Accuracy

Accuracy is the most straightforward metric, especially for classification problems. It is the ratio of correct predictions to total predictions.

Accuracy=Number of Correct PredictionsTotal Number of Predictions\text{Accuracy} = \frac{\text{Number of Correct Predictions}}{\text{Total Number of Predictions}}Accuracy=Total Number of PredictionsNumber of Correct Predictions

2. Precision

Precision measures the accuracy of positive predictions. In classification, it tells us the proportion of true positive predictions out of all predicted positives.

Precision=TPTP+FP\text{Precision} = \frac{TP}{TP + FP}Precision=TP+FPTP

Where:

- TPTPTP = True Positive
- FPFPFP = False Positive

3. Recall (Sensitivity or True Positive Rate)

Recall measures the ability of the model to correctly identify positive instances. It tells us the proportion of actual positives that were correctly identified by the model.

Recall=TPTP+FN\text{Recall} = \frac{TP}{TP + FN}Recall=TP+FNTP

Where:

- TPTPTP = True Positive
- FNFNFN = False Negative

4. F1-Score

F1-score is the harmonic mean of precision and recall. It is especially useful when there is a need to balance precision and recall.

F1-Score=2×Precision×RecallPrecision+RecallF1\text{-Score} = 2 \times \frac{\text{Precision} \times \text{Recall}}{\text{Precision} + \text{Recall}}F1-Score=2×Precision+RecallPrecision×Recall

5. Confusion Matrix

A **confusion matrix** is a summary table used to assess the performance of a classification model, providing insights into the types of errors the model is making (false positives, false negatives).

Summary

In this chapter, we:

- Explored the fundamentals of **supervised learning**, including **regression** and **classification** tasks.
- Built a **linear regression model** for predicting continuous values.
- Created a **classification model** using **decision trees** to predict categorical outcomes.
- Discussed important **evaluation metrics** such as **accuracy**, **precision**, **recall**, and **F1-score** to assess model performance.

Supervised learning is a powerful tool for building predictive models. In the next chapter, we will dive into **unsupervised learning** and explore techniques like **K-Means clustering** for grouping data.

CHAPTER 6

DIVING INTO UNSUPERVISED

LEARNING

Unsupervised learning is one of the key categories of machine learning. Unlike **supervised learning**, where models are trained on labeled data, **unsupervised learning** involves learning from data without labels. The goal of unsupervised learning is often to uncover hidden patterns, group similar items, or reduce the complexity of data without predefined outcomes. In this chapter, we will explore the basics of unsupervised learning, focusing on clustering and anomaly detection techniques. We will dive deeper into **K-Means clustering** and **Dimensionality Reduction** techniques like **Principal Component Analysis (PCA)**, as well as applying clustering to a real-world problem like customer segmentation.

6.1 What is Unsupervised Learning?

Unsupervised Learning refers to the machine learning tasks where the algorithm is trained on unlabeled data. The model is not provided with output labels for the data points, and instead, it tries to find inherent patterns or groupings in the data.

Key Types of Unsupervised Learning:

1. **Clustering**: This is the process of grouping data points into clusters, where data points within each cluster are more similar to each other than to those in other clusters.
   - Example: Grouping customers based on their purchasing behavior.
2. **Anomaly Detection**: In this task, the goal is to identify rare or abnormal data points that deviate significantly from the rest of the data.
   - **Example**: Detecting fraudulent transactions in a bank's transaction records.

Applications of Unsupervised Learning:

- **Market Segmentation**: Grouping customers based on purchasing behavior to personalize marketing campaigns.

- **Data Compression**: Reducing the size of data while retaining important features.

- **Anomaly Detection**: Identifying unusual patterns in data, such as fraud detection in credit card transactions.

- **Feature Extraction**: Identifying relevant features from a large set of data for use in supervised learning models.

6.2 K-Means Clustering: Building a Simple Clustering Model to Group Data

K-Means clustering is one of the most popular and widely used clustering algorithms. The goal of K-Means is to partition the data into KKK clusters where each data point belongs to the cluster with the nearest mean. The algorithm minimizes the variance within each cluster by iteratively updating the cluster centroids.

How K-Means Works:

1. **Initialization**: Choose KKK initial cluster centroids randomly from the data.
2. **Assignment Step**: Assign each data point to the nearest centroid.
3. **Update Step**: Calculate new centroids by taking the mean of all points assigned to each cluster.
4. **Repeat**: Repeat the assignment and update steps until the centroids no longer change significantly (convergence).

Step-by-Step Implementation of K-Means Clustering:

Let's implement K-Means clustering using the **Iris dataset**, which contains data about different iris flowers (with features like petal length, petal width, and sepal length). Our goal is to cluster the flowers based on these features.

python

```python
import numpy as np
import pandas as pd
from sklearn.datasets import load_iris
from sklearn.cluster import KMeans
import matplotlib.pyplot as plt
```

```
# Load the Iris dataset
iris = load_iris()
X = iris.data  # Features

# Create the K-Means model
kmeans = KMeans(n_clusters=3, random_state=42)

# Fit the model
kmeans.fit(X)

# Get the cluster labels for each data point
labels = kmeans.labels_

# Get the coordinates of the cluster centers
centroids = kmeans.cluster_centers_

# Plot the clusters
plt.scatter(X[:,   0],   X[:,   1],   c=labels,
cmap='viridis')
plt.scatter(centroids[:,   0],   centroids[:,   1],
marker='x', s=200, c='red')
plt.xlabel('Sepal Length')
plt.ylabel('Sepal Width')
plt.title('K-Means Clustering of Iris Dataset')
plt.show()
```

In this example:

- We perform K-Means clustering with K=3K=3K=3, as the Iris dataset contains three classes of flowers.

- The `labels_` attribute gives the cluster assignments for each flower, and `cluster_centers_` provides the centroids of the clusters.

- We then visualize the clusters and centroids on a scatter plot.

Key Points:

- The K-Means algorithm works best when the data points naturally form distinct clusters.

- Choosing the correct value for KKK is crucial. A common method for selecting KKK is the **elbow method**, where you plot the sum of squared errors for different values of KKK and choose the KKK at which the rate of decrease sharply slows.

6.3 Dimensionality Reduction: Techniques Like PCA (Principal Component Analysis) to Reduce the Complexity of Data

As datasets grow in size and complexity, it becomes increasingly difficult to process and analyze them effectively. **Dimensionality reduction** is a technique used to reduce the number of features (variables) in a dataset while retaining as much of the important information as possible. This can help improve the efficiency and performance of machine learning models.

Principal Component Analysis (PCA):

PCA is one of the most popular techniques for dimensionality reduction. It works by identifying the directions (principal components) in which the data varies the most and projecting the data onto a lower-dimensional space along those directions. By doing this, PCA reduces the number of features while preserving the essential patterns in the data.

How PCA Works:

1. **Standardize the data**: Ensure each feature has zero mean and unit variance.
2. **Compute the covariance matrix**: The covariance matrix tells us how the features of the dataset relate to each other.
3. **Find the eigenvalues and eigenvectors**: These represent the directions of maximum variance.

4. **Project the data onto the new principal components**: This creates a lower-dimensional representation of the data.

Step-by-Step Implementation of PCA:

Let's apply PCA to the Iris dataset to reduce its dimensions from 4 to 2.

```python
from sklearn.decomposition import PCA

# Standardize the data
from sklearn.preprocessing import StandardScaler
X_scaled = StandardScaler().fit_transform(X)

# Apply PCA to reduce dimensions from 4 to 2
pca = PCA(n_components=2)
X_pca = pca.fit_transform(X_scaled)

# Visualize the reduced data
plt.scatter(X_pca[:,    0],    X_pca[:,    1],
c=iris.target, cmap='viridis')
plt.xlabel('Principal Component 1')
plt.ylabel('Principal Component 2')
plt.title('PCA of Iris Dataset')
plt.show()
```

In this code:

- We first scale the features using **StandardScaler** to ensure they all have the same mean and variance.
- Then, we apply **PCA** to reduce the data from 4 dimensions to 2.
- Finally, we plot the transformed data to visualize it in the reduced space.

Key Points:

- PCA helps to simplify datasets with many features, making it easier to visualize and analyze.
- It is commonly used as a preprocessing step before applying machine learning algorithms to high-dimensional data.

6.4 Real-World Application: Using Clustering to Segment Customers Based on Purchasing Behavior

Let's now apply **K-Means clustering** to a real-world dataset: **customer purchasing behavior**. Our goal is to segment customers into different groups based on their spending habits, which can then be used for targeted marketing.

Step-by-Step Implementation:

Imagine we have a dataset with information about customers' annual income and spending score (based on their purchase behavior). We want to group them into distinct segments.

python

```python
import pandas as pd
from sklearn.cluster import KMeans
import matplotlib.pyplot as plt

# Simulated customer data
data = {'CustomerID': [1, 2, 3, 4, 5, 6, 7, 8, 9, 10],
        'AnnualIncome': [15, 16, 17, 18, 19, 20, 21, 22, 23, 24],
        'SpendingScore': [39, 81, 6, 77, 40, 76, 94, 3, 72, 88]}

df = pd.DataFrame(data)

# Select the features for clustering
X = df[['AnnualIncome', 'SpendingScore']]
```

```
# Apply K-Means Clustering
kmeans = KMeans(n_clusters=3, random_state=42)
df['Cluster'] = kmeans.fit_predict(X)

# Plot the clusters
plt.scatter(df['AnnualIncome'],
df['SpendingScore'],          c=df['Cluster'],
cmap='viridis')
plt.xlabel('Annual Income')
plt.ylabel('Spending Score')
plt.title('Customer    Segmentation    Based    on
Purchasing Behavior')
plt.show()
```

In this example:

- We use **K-Means clustering** to group customers based on their annual income and spending score.
- The resulting clusters represent different customer segments, which can be useful for personalized marketing strategies.

Key Points:

- **Clustering** can reveal patterns in data that are not immediately obvious, allowing businesses to identify distinct customer segments or product preferences.

- Customer segmentation is just one application of clustering; it can be used in a wide range of industries, such as finance, healthcare, and retail.

Summary

In this chapter, we:

- Explored **unsupervised learning**, focusing on clustering and anomaly detection.
- Learned how **K-Means clustering** works and implemented it to group data points into clusters.
- Introduced **PCA (Principal Component Analysis)** as a technique for reducing the dimensionality of complex datasets.
- Applied clustering to a **real-world dataset** for customer segmentation, illustrating how unsupervised learning can be used to gain insights into customer behavior.

Unsupervised learning provides powerful tools for discovering hidden structures in data. In the next chapter, we will dive into **supervised learning** techniques in more detail, focusing on classification and regression tasks.

CHAPTER 7

INTRODUCTION TO NEURAL NETWORKS

Neural networks are a foundational concept in deep learning and artificial intelligence (AI). Inspired by the human brain, neural networks consist of interconnected layers of nodes (or neurons) that work together to process data and make predictions. In this chapter, we will explore the basics of neural networks, how they mimic the human brain, and their role in solving complex AI problems. We will also look at the architecture of neural networks, including neurons, layers, and activation functions. Finally, we will walk through the process of building your very first neural network using **Keras** or **TensorFlow**.

7.1 What is a Neural Network?

A **neural network** is a computational model inspired by the way biological neurons in the human brain process information. Just like the brain, a neural network learns from data, adjusts its internal parameters, and improves its ability to make predictions or classifications over time.

Neural networks are used in a wide variety of AI applications, including:

- **Image Recognition**: Identifying objects or patterns in images.
- **Natural Language Processing (NLP)**: Understanding and generating human language.
- **Recommendation Systems**: Suggesting products, movies, or music based on user behavior.
- **Autonomous Vehicles**: Helping self-driving cars understand their environment.

Basic Concept:

A neural network takes an **input**, processes it through multiple layers of **neurons**, and produces an **output**. During training, the network adjusts its parameters to minimize the error between its predictions and the actual results (labels), improving its ability to make accurate predictions on new, unseen data.

7.2 Neurons and Layers: Understanding Layers, Neurons, and How Information Flows Through a Network

A neural network consists of layers of **neurons** (or nodes), where each neuron is connected to other neurons in adjacent layers. These connections are represented by **weights**, which are learned during training. The information flows through the network from the input layer to the output layer.

1. Neurons

Each neuron in a neural network is similar to a biological neuron in the brain. It receives input, performs a computation, and produces an output that is passed to the next layer. The core components of a neuron are:

- **Inputs**: The features or data points provided to the neuron.
- **Weights**: The importance assigned to each input.
- **Bias**: An additional parameter that helps the model make better predictions.
- **Output**: The result of applying an activation function to the weighted sum of inputs.

2. Layers

A neural network is composed of three main types of layers:

- **Input Layer**: The first layer that receives the data. Each neuron in this layer represents one feature of the input data.
- **Hidden Layers**: Intermediate layers where the network processes information and learns patterns. These layers are not directly exposed to the output.
- **Output Layer**: The final layer that produces the prediction or classification result.

Information flows through the network in the following manner:

1. **Input Layer**: Receives the raw data and passes it to the first hidden layer.
2. **Hidden Layers**: Each hidden layer processes the data, transforming it and passing it to the next layer.
3. **Output Layer**: Produces the final prediction or classification.

3. Weights and Biases

- **Weights**: Each connection between neurons has an associated weight, which controls the importance of that connection in the learning process. Weights are adjusted during training to minimize error.

- **Bias**: The bias term allows the model to make better predictions by shifting the activation function, helping the model learn patterns that are not centered around zero.

7.3 Activation Functions: The Role of Activation Functions in Neural Networks

Activation functions are mathematical functions applied to the output of each neuron to introduce non-linearity into the network. Non-linearity is crucial because real-world data is often non-linear, and linear models are insufficient for solving complex tasks like image recognition or natural language understanding.

Common Activation Functions:

1. **Sigmoid Function**:

- o The **sigmoid** function maps values between 0 and 1.
- o It is commonly used in the output layer of binary classification models.
- o Formula:

$\sigma(x)=11+e-x\sigma(x)$ $=$ $\frac{1}{1}$ $+$ e^{-x} $\sigma(x)=1+e-x1$

- o It squashes input values into a small range, which can lead to problems with vanishing gradients.

2. **ReLU (Rectified Linear Unit)**:
- o The **ReLU** function is the most widely used activation function for hidden layers in neural networks.
- o It outputs the input directly if it is positive; otherwise, it outputs zero.
- o Formula:

$ReLU(x)=max(0,x)\text{ReLU}(x)$ $=$ $\max(0, x)ReLU(x)=max(0,x)$

- o ReLU is computationally efficient and helps prevent the vanishing gradient problem.

3. **Tanh (Hyperbolic Tangent)**:

- o The **tanh** function maps values between -1 and 1.
- o Formula:

$$\tanh(x) = \frac{2}{1 + e^{-2x}} - 1$$

- o Like the sigmoid function, but it outputs values with a wider range, improving performance in some cases.

4. **Softmax Function**:
   - o The **softmax** function is often used in the output layer of multi-class classification models.
   - o It converts logits (raw predictions) into probabilities by normalizing the output.
   - o Formula:

$$\text{Softmax}(x_i) = \frac{e^{x_i}}{\sum_{j} e^{x_j}}$$

- o It ensures that the output values sum up to 1, which is essential for classification tasks.

Why Activation Functions Are Important:

- They introduce **non-linearity**, allowing the neural network to learn complex patterns in the data.
- Without activation functions, the network would be just a linear model, regardless of how many layers it has.

7.4 Building Your First Neural Network: Using Keras or TensorFlow to Build a Simple Neural Network for Classification

Now that we understand the basics of neural networks, let's build a simple neural network model using **Keras** or **TensorFlow**, two of the most popular deep learning libraries in Python. For this example, we will build a neural network to classify images from the **MNIST dataset**, which contains images of handwritten digits (0-9).

1. Installing Required Libraries

First, ensure you have the necessary libraries installed. You can install **Keras** (which uses TensorFlow as a backend) by running:

bash

```
pip install tensorflow
```

2. Importing Libraries and Dataset

```
python
```

```
import tensorflow as tf
from tensorflow.keras.models import Sequential
from    tensorflow.keras.layers    import    Dense,
Flatten
from tensorflow.keras.datasets import mnist
from          tensorflow.keras.utils          import
to_categorical

# Load the MNIST dataset
(X_train,    y_train),    (X_test,    y_test)    =
mnist.load_data()

# Normalize the data to be between 0 and 1
X_train, X_test = X_train / 255.0, X_test / 255.0

# One-hot encode the labels
y_train = to_categorical(y_train, 10)
y_test = to_categorical(y_test, 10)
```

In this code:

- We load the **MNIST dataset**, which contains 60,000 training images and 10,000 test images of handwritten digits.

100

- We normalize the pixel values by dividing by 255, ensuring that all values are between 0 and 1.
- We use **one-hot encoding** to convert the target labels (digits 0-9) into a format suitable for classification.

3. Building the Neural Network Model

We will build a simple feed-forward neural network with one hidden layer. The network will use **ReLU** for the hidden layer and **Softmax** for the output layer.

python

```
# Build the neural network model
model = Sequential([
    Flatten(input_shape=(28, 28)),  # Flatten the
28x28 images into a 1D vector
    Dense(128, activation='relu'),    # Hidden
layer with 128 neurons and ReLU activation
    Dense(10, activation='softmax')   # Output
layer with 10 neurons (one for each digit)
])

# Compile the model
model.compile(optimizer='adam',
loss='categorical_crossentropy',
metrics=['accuracy'])
```

In this code:

- The `Flatten` layer converts the 28x28 pixel images into a 1D vector of 784 values.
- The `Dense` layer with 128 neurons applies the **ReLU** activation function.
- The final `Dense` layer has 10 neurons (one for each digit) and uses the **Softmax** activation function for multi-class classification.

4. Training the Model

Now, let's train the model using the training data.

python

```python
# Train the model
model.fit(X_train,      y_train,      epochs=5,
batch_size=32, validation_data=(X_test, y_test))
```

In this code:

- We train the model for 5 epochs, using a batch size of 32 samples per iteration.
- The model is validated on the test set during training to monitor its performance on unseen data.

5. Evaluating the Model

After training, we can evaluate the model on the test set to see how well it performs.

python

```
# Evaluate the model on the test set
test_loss, test_acc = model.evaluate(X_test, y_test)
print(f"Test accuracy: {test_acc * 100:.2f}%")
```

6. Making Predictions

Finally, we can use the trained model to make predictions on new data.

python

```
# Make predictions on the test set
predictions = model.predict(X_test)

# Print the predicted class for the first image
print(f"Predicted                    label: {predictions[0].argmax()}")
```

Summary

In this chapter, we:

- Explored the concept of **neural networks** and their inspiration from the human brain.
- Learned about the structure of neural networks, including **neurons**, **layers**, and **activation functions**.
- Built a **simple neural network** for **classification** using **Keras** and **TensorFlow** to classify handwritten digits from the MNIST dataset.
- Discussed the importance of **ReLU** and **Softmax** activation functions for hidden and output layers, respectively.

Neural networks are at the core of many modern AI applications. In the next chapter, we will dive deeper into **deep learning** and explore more advanced architectures like **Convolutional Neural Networks (CNNs)** for image recognition tasks.

CHAPTER 8

DEEP LEARNING BASICS

Deep Learning is a subfield of **Machine Learning (ML)** that focuses on algorithms inspired by the structure and function of the **brain's neural networks**. While machine learning models typically use simpler algorithms to analyze data, deep learning models employ large, multi-layered networks to learn complex patterns from large datasets. Deep learning is particularly effective in tasks involving unstructured data, such as images, text, and audio.

In this chapter, we will explore the basics of deep learning, including its differences from traditional machine learning. We will introduce key deep learning architectures like **Convolutional Neural Networks (CNNs)** for image recognition and **Recurrent Neural Networks (RNNs)** for sequence data, such as text or time series. Finally, we will walk through building a simple deep learning model using **Keras** or **TensorFlow**.

8.1 What is Deep Learning? Differences Between Deep Learning and Machine Learning

Deep Learning is a subset of machine learning that uses **artificial neural networks** with many layers (hence the term "deep"). Deep learning models are designed to automatically learn hierarchical representations of data, allowing them to recognize complex patterns and features.

Key Differences Between Machine Learning and Deep Learning:

Feature	Machine Learning	Deep Learning
Algorithm Complexity	Simpler algorithms, like linear regression, decision trees	Uses neural networks with many layers (deep neural networks)
Feature Engineering	Requires manual feature extraction and selection	Learns features automatically from data
Data Requirements	Works well with smaller datasets (hundreds to thousands of samples)	Requires large datasets (millions of samples)

Feature	Machine Learning	Deep Learning
Computational Resources	Can run on standard CPUs	Requires GPUs for efficient training, especially for large datasets
Task Complexity	Best for simpler problems like classification or regression	Best for complex problems like image recognition, speech recognition, and natural language processing

Deep learning is particularly powerful when working with high-dimensional data like images and natural language, where traditional machine learning models struggle to extract meaningful features.

8.2 Convolutional Neural Networks (CNNs): Introduction to CNNs for Image Recognition

Convolutional Neural Networks (CNNs) are a class of deep learning algorithms specifically designed for processing data that has a grid-like topology, such as images. CNNs excel at image-related tasks because they

107

automatically learn spatial hierarchies of features, reducing the need for manual feature extraction.

How CNNs Work:

1. **Convolutional Layers**: These layers apply filters (or kernels) to the input image. The filters are used to detect basic features like edges, corners, and textures in the image. The output of this operation is a feature map.

2. **Activation Functions**: After each convolution operation, the output is passed through an **activation function** (typically **ReLU**) to introduce non-linearity.

3. **Pooling Layers**: Pooling (usually **max pooling**) is applied to reduce the spatial dimensions of the feature maps. This makes the network more efficient and helps to prevent overfitting.

4. **Fully Connected Layers**: After several convolutional and pooling layers, the network typically has one or more fully connected layers that make final predictions based on the features extracted by the previous layers.

CNN Architecture Example:

- **Input Layer**: The raw image data.
- **Convolutional Layers**: These extract important features from the image.
- **Pooling Layers**: Reduce the size of the feature maps.
- **Fully Connected Layers**: Connect all neurons and make the final classification.
- **Output Layer**: The final prediction (e.g., class of the image).

Example CNN for Image Classification:

python

```
from tensorflow.keras.models import Sequential
from tensorflow.keras.layers import Conv2D,
MaxPooling2D, Flatten, Dense
from tensorflow.keras.datasets import cifar10

# Load the CIFAR-10 dataset (60,000 32x32 color
images in 10 classes)
(X_train,    y_train),    (X_test,    y_test)    =
cifar10.load_data()

# Normalize the data
X_train, X_test = X_train / 255.0, X_test / 255.0

# Build the CNN model
```

```
model = Sequential([
    Conv2D(32,    (3,    3),    activation='relu',
input_shape=(32, 32, 3)),   # Convolutional layer
    MaxPooling2D((2, 2)),   # Pooling layer
    Conv2D(64,  (3,  3),  activation='relu'),    #
Another convolutional layer
    MaxPooling2D((2, 2)),   # Pooling layer
    Flatten(),   # Flatten the 3D outputs to 1D
    Dense(64,    activation='relu'),      #    Fully
connected layer
    Dense(10,  activation='softmax')    #  Output
layer (10 classes)
])

# Compile the model
model.compile(optimizer='adam',
loss='sparse_categorical_crossentropy',
metrics=['accuracy'])

# Train the model
model.fit(X_train,      y_train,      epochs=5,
validation_data=(X_test, y_test))
```

In this example:

- We use **CIFAR-10**, a dataset of 32x32 images with 10 classes.
- We define a CNN model with convolutional layers for feature extraction, pooling layers for

dimensionality reduction, and fully connected layers for classification.

- The model is trained using the **Adam optimizer** and **sparse categorical cross-entropy loss**.

CNNs are highly effective for image recognition tasks because they preserve spatial hierarchies and reduce the complexity of feature extraction.

8.3 Recurrent Neural Networks (RNNs): Understanding RNNs for Sequence Data

Recurrent Neural Networks (RNNs) are a class of neural networks designed for sequential data, where the order of the data points matters. Unlike traditional neural networks, RNNs have connections that form cycles, allowing information to persist from one step to the next in the sequence.

How RNNs Work:

- **Sequential Data**: RNNs are suited for tasks like time series forecasting, natural language processing (NLP), and speech recognition, where the data consists of sequences (e.g., words in a sentence or stock prices over time).

- **Hidden State**: RNNs maintain a "hidden state" that captures information about the previous steps in the sequence, which is updated as new data points are processed.

- **Feedback Loops**: RNNs pass information from one step to the next, allowing them to learn dependencies in the data over time.

Limitations of Vanilla RNNs:

Vanilla RNNs struggle to capture long-term dependencies because they suffer from the **vanishing gradient problem**, where gradients (used for model training) can become very small as they propagate back through many time steps.

Long Short-Term Memory (LSTM) and Gated Recurrent Units (GRU) are advanced types of RNNs designed to overcome the vanishing gradient problem and capture longer dependencies.

Example of an RNN for Text Generation:

Here's how to build a simple RNN model for **text generation** using **Keras**:

python

```python
from tensorflow.keras.models import Sequential
from tensorflow.keras.layers import SimpleRNN,
Dense, Embedding
from tensorflow.keras.optimizers import Adam
from tensorflow.keras.preprocessing.text import
Tokenizer
from      tensorflow.keras.preprocessing.sequence
import pad_sequences

# Example text data
texts = ["I love machine learning", "Deep
learning is amazing", "AI is the future"]

# Tokenize the text data
tokenizer = Tokenizer()
tokenizer.fit_on_texts(texts)
sequences = tokenizer.texts_to_sequences(texts)

# Pad sequences to ensure equal length
X = pad_sequences(sequences, padding='post')

# Build the RNN model
model = Sequential([

Embedding(input_dim=len(tokenizer.word_index)  +
1, output_dim=10, input_length=X.shape[1]),
    SimpleRNN(64, activation='relu'),
```

```
    Dense(len(tokenizer.word_index)       +      1,
activation='softmax')   # Output  layer  for  text
generation
])

# Compile the model
model.compile(optimizer=Adam(),
loss='sparse_categorical_crossentropy',
metrics=['accuracy'])

# Train  the  model  (dummy  example  with  minimal
data)
model.fit(X,  X,  epochs=10)
```

In this example:

- We tokenize and pad text data, then build a simple RNN for text generation using an **Embedding layer** (to convert words into dense vectors), a **SimpleRNN layer**, and a **Dense layer** for generating text.
- While this is a simplified example, real-world RNNs like **LSTMs** or **GRUs** would be used for more advanced text tasks like language modeling or machine translation.

RNNs are ideal for processing sequential data, where the order of elements is critical.

8.4 Building a Simple Deep Learning Model: Hands-on Implementation Using Keras/TensorFlow

Now that we understand the basics of CNNs and RNNs, let's build a simple **deep learning model** using **Keras** and **TensorFlow**. We'll use a **fully connected neural network** for binary classification on a small dataset.

Step-by-Step Implementation:

python

```python
import tensorflow as tf
from tensorflow.keras.models import Sequential
from tensorflow.keras.layers import Dense
from        tensorflow.keras.datasets       import
binary_classification_data  # Example dataset

# Load the dataset
(X_train,    y_train),    (X_test,    y_test)    =
binary_classification_data.load_data()

# Build the neural network model
model = Sequential([
    Dense(64,                    activation='relu',
input_shape=(X_train.shape[1],)),
    Dense(32, activation='relu'),
    Dense(1,  activation='sigmoid')    #  Output
layer for binary classification
```

115

```
])

# Compile the model
model.compile(optimizer='adam',
loss='binary_crossentropy',
metrics=['accuracy'])

# Train the model
model.fit(X_train,      y_train,      epochs=10,
batch_size=32, validation_data=(X_test, y_test))
```

In this example:

- We use a **simple feed-forward neural network** with two hidden layers (64 and 32 neurons, ReLU activation) and a **sigmoid output layer** for binary classification.
- The **binary crossentropy** loss function is used for classification tasks with two classes (e.g., 0 or 1).
- We train the model for 10 epochs, using a batch size of 32, and validate on the test data.

Summary

In this chapter, we:

- Learned the basics of **deep learning**, understanding how deep neural networks differ from traditional machine learning models.

- Explored **Convolutional Neural Networks (CNNs)** for image recognition tasks and how they automatically extract features from images.

- Introduced **Recurrent Neural Networks (RNNs)** for handling sequential data, such as text and time series, and learned about advanced RNN architectures like **LSTMs**.

- Built a simple **deep learning model** using **Keras/TensorFlow**, applying a neural network for binary classification.

Deep learning is a powerful tool, especially for tasks involving large amounts of unstructured data, like images and text. In the next chapter, we will dive into advanced topics in deep learning, such as **transfer learning** and **model optimization**.

CHAPTER 9

NATURAL LANGUAGE

PROCESSING (NLP)

Natural Language Processing (NLP) is a subfield of Artificial Intelligence (AI) that focuses on the interaction between computers and human language. NLP involves enabling machines to understand, interpret, and generate human language in a way that is both valuable and meaningful. This chapter will provide an introduction to NLP, explore common preprocessing techniques, and guide you through building a text classification model, such as **sentiment analysis**. Finally, we will look at **pretrained models** like **BERT** and **GPT** and how they are used in modern NLP tasks.

9.1 What is NLP? Introduction to NLP and Its Real-World Applications

Natural Language Processing is a powerful tool that enables machines to understand and generate human language. NLP combines computational linguistics (which involves rule-based modeling of human language) with machine learning and deep learning models to process and analyze large amounts of natural language data.

Key Applications of NLP:

1. **Chatbots and Virtual Assistants**:
     - Chatbots like **Siri**, **Google Assistant**, and **Alexa** rely heavily on NLP to understand user commands and respond in natural language.
     - These systems perform tasks like setting reminders, answering questions, and controlling smart devices.
2. **Sentiment Analysis**:
     - **Sentiment analysis** involves determining the sentiment behind a piece of text, such as whether a tweet, review, or comment is positive, negative, or neutral. It's used

119

extensively in social media monitoring and customer feedback analysis.

3. **Machine Translation**:
   o NLP is used to translate text from one language to another, such as **Google Translate** or **DeepL**. These systems rely on sophisticated models to capture the meanings of words and phrases in context.

4. **Text Summarization**:
   o NLP can automatically generate summaries of long documents or articles. This is particularly useful for summarizing news articles, academic papers, or business reports.

5. **Information Retrieval**:
   o NLP is used in search engines like **Google**, which process user queries to retrieve relevant information. These systems use techniques like **TF-IDF** and **word embeddings** to match search queries with relevant documents.

6. **Speech Recognition**:
   o Speech recognition systems, such as **speech-to-text**, convert spoken language into written

text, enabling voice commands and transcription services.

NLP plays a significant role in everyday technologies and is becoming more integrated into applications that require human-computer interaction.

9.2 Text Preprocessing: Tokenization, Stop Words, Stemming, and Lemmatization

Before we build NLP models, we need to preprocess the text data to convert it into a format that can be efficiently processed by machine learning models. Preprocessing involves several key steps:

1. Tokenization:

Tokenization is the process of breaking down text into smaller units, called **tokens**. Tokens can be words, sentences, or even characters. Tokenization is a crucial first step in most NLP tasks because it transforms raw text into a structured form that can be used for analysis.

Example:

```python
from nltk.tokenize import word_tokenize

text = "I love learning about machine learning!"
tokens = word_tokenize(text)
print(tokens)
```

Output:

```python
['I', 'love', 'learning', 'about', 'machine',
'learning', '!']
```

2. Stop Words Removal:

Stop words are common words (such as "the", "a", "in", etc.) that don't add much meaning to the text and can be safely removed. Removing stop words helps reduce the dimensionality of the data and improves the model's efficiency.

Example:

```python
from nltk.corpus import stopwords

stop_words = set(stopwords.words('english'))
```

```
filtered_tokens = [word for word in tokens if
word.lower() not in stop_words]
print(filtered_tokens)
```

Output:

```
python
```

```
['love', 'learning', 'machine', 'learning', '!']
```

3. Stemming:

Stemming is the process of reducing words to their root form by removing prefixes and suffixes. For example, "running" becomes "run". While it is useful for some tasks, it can sometimes lead to non-dictionary words.

Example:

```
python
```

```
from nltk.stem import PorterStemmer

stemmer = PorterStemmer()
stemmed_words = [stemmer.stem(word) for word in
filtered_tokens]
print(stemmed_words)
```

Output:

```
python
```

```
['love', 'learn', 'machin', 'learn', '!']
```
4. Lemmatization:

Lemmatization is similar to stemming, but it returns the base or dictionary form of a word (called a **lemma**). It uses a vocabulary and context to transform words into their correct form. Lemmatization is more accurate than stemming because it considers the word's meaning.

Example:

```
python
```

```
from nltk.stem import WordNetLemmatizer

lemmatizer = WordNetLemmatizer()
lemmatized_words = [lemmatizer.lemmatize(word)
for word in filtered_tokens]
print(lemmatized_words)
```

Output:

```
python
```

```
['love', 'learning', 'machine', 'learning', '!']
```

Lemmatization is typically preferred for most NLP tasks because it provides more meaningful reductions of words.

9.3 Building a Text Classification Model: Implementing Sentiment Analysis Using Machine Learning Techniques

Now that we've preprocessed the text data, let's build a **text classification model** for sentiment analysis. The goal of sentiment analysis is to classify text as **positive**, **negative**, or **neutral** based on its content. We'll use **Scikit-learn** for this task.

Step 1: Importing Libraries and Dataset

Let's assume we have a dataset of product reviews labeled as positive or negative. First, we import the necessary libraries and load the data.

```python
import pandas as pd
from sklearn.model_selection import train_test_split
from sklearn.feature_extraction.text import TfidfVectorizer
from sklearn.naive_bayes import MultinomialNB
```

```
from sklearn.metrics import accuracy_score

# Example dataset (text and labels: 1 for
positive, 0 for negative)
data = {'text': ['I love this product', 'This is
terrible', 'Best purchase ever', 'Very bad
quality'],
        'label': [1, 0, 1, 0]}
df = pd.DataFrame(data)

# Split the data into training and testing sets
X_train, X_test, y_train, y_test =
train_test_split(df['text'], df['label'],
test_size=0.25, random_state=42)
```

Step 2: Text Vectorization

We need to convert the raw text data into numerical vectors that machine learning models can process. One popular method for text vectorization is **TF-IDF** (Term Frequency-Inverse Document Frequency), which reflects the importance of words in a document relative to the entire dataset.

```
python
```

```
# Create a TF-IDF vectorizer and transform the
text data
```

```
vectorizer                                    =
TfidfVectorizer(stop_words='english')
X_train_tfidf                                 =
vectorizer.fit_transform(X_train)
X_test_tfidf = vectorizer.transform(X_test)
```

Step 3: Training the Model

Next, we train a **Multinomial Naive Bayes** classifier, a commonly used model for text classification tasks.

python

```
# Train a Naive Bayes model
model = MultinomialNB()
model.fit(X_train_tfidf, y_train)
```

Step 4: Making Predictions and Evaluating the Model

Finally, we use the trained model to make predictions on the test set and evaluate its performance.

python

```
# Make predictions on the test set
y_pred = model.predict(X_test_tfidf)

# Evaluate the model's accuracy
accuracy = accuracy_score(y_test, y_pred)
print(f"Accuracy: {accuracy * 100:.2f}%")
```

In this example, we performed **sentiment analysis** to classify reviews as positive or negative. The model was evaluated using accuracy, which is the percentage of correctly classified samples.

9.4 Using Pretrained Models: How to Use Pre-Trained Models Like BERT or GPT for NLP Tasks

While training a model from scratch can be useful, it is often more efficient to use **pretrained models** for NLP tasks. Pretrained models are neural networks that have already been trained on large datasets, and they can be fine-tuned for specific tasks like sentiment analysis or text summarization.

1.   BERT   (Bidirectional   Encoder   Representations   from Transformers)

BERT is a transformer-based model developed by Google, which is pretrained on large text corpora and can be fine-tuned for specific NLP tasks. BERT is capable of understanding the context of words in both directions (left-to-right and right-to-left), making it particularly effective for tasks like question answering, named entity recognition, and sentiment analysis.

128

2. GPT (Generative Pretrained Transformer)

GPT is another transformer-based model, developed by OpenAI. GPT is trained to generate human-like text and can be fine-tuned for tasks like text generation, summarization, and translation. GPT models are used for creative applications, such as writing essays, generating poetry, or even programming.

Using BERT for Text Classification:

To use a pretrained BERT model for text classification, we can leverage the **Transformers** library by Hugging Face.

```python
from transformers import BertTokenizer,
BertForSequenceClassification
from transformers import Trainer,
TrainingArguments

# Load the pretrained BERT model and tokenizer
tokenizer = BertTokenizer.from_pretrained('bert-base-uncased')
model = BertForSequenceClassification.from_pretrained('bert-base-uncased')
```

```
# Tokenize the text data
inputs       =       tokenizer(df['text'].tolist(),
padding=True,                    truncation=True,
return_tensors='pt')

# Fine-tune the model (simplified example)
training_args                              =
TrainingArguments(output_dir='./results',
num_train_epochs=3)
trainer            =            Trainer(model=model,
args=training_args, train_dataset=inputs)
trainer.train()
```

Using pretrained models like **BERT** or **GPT** provides state-of-the-art performance on NLP tasks and dramatically reduces the time and resources required to train a model from scratch.

Summary

In this chapter, we:

- Explored the basics of **Natural Language Processing (NLP)** and its real-world applications, including **chatbots**, **sentiment analysis**, and **machine translation**.

- Learned about key **text preprocessing** techniques, including **tokenization**, **stop word removal**, **stemming**, and **lemmatization**, which are essential steps in preparing text data for machine learning models.

- Built a **text classification model** for **sentiment analysis** using traditional machine learning techniques with **Scikit-learn**.

- Examined the power of **pretrained models** like **BERT** and **GPT**, which can be fine-tuned for various NLP tasks to save time and resources while achieving state-of-the-art results.

NLP is a crucial part of AI, and mastering it opens up numerous possibilities for building intelligent systems that can understand and generate human language. In the next chapter, we will dive deeper into **unsupervised learning** and explore clustering techniques like **K-Means** for grouping similar data points.

CHAPTER 10

INTRODUCTION TO COMPUTER VISION

Computer Vision (CV) is a subfield of Artificial Intelligence (AI) that enables machines to interpret and understand the visual world. It involves developing algorithms that allow computers to process and analyze digital images or videos to extract meaningful information. From identifying objects in images to recognizing faces and interpreting video content, computer vision plays a crucial role in various applications, including self-driving cars, medical imaging, and facial recognition systems.

In this chapter, we will introduce the basics of computer vision, explore common image preprocessing techniques, and guide you through building an image classification model using **Convolutional Neural Networks (CNNs)**. Finally, we will delve into more advanced computer vision tasks such as **object detection** and **image segmentation**, which are essential for applications in industries like healthcare, security, and robotics.

10.1 What is Computer Vision? Understanding the Field of Computer Vision and Its Applications

Computer vision refers to the ability of machines to interpret and make decisions based on visual data. The goal is to develop algorithms that can mimic the way humans perceive and process visual information.

Key Tasks in Computer Vision:

1. **Image Classification**: Categorizing an image into one of several predefined classes. For example, classifying images of animals into categories like cats, dogs, and birds.

2. **Object Detection**: Identifying and locating objects within an image. This involves both classification and localization of objects.

3. **Image Segmentation**: Dividing an image into regions or segments, typically by identifying different objects or areas within the image.

133

4. **Facial Recognition**: Identifying or verifying individuals based on facial features in an image or video.

5. **Optical Character Recognition (OCR)**: Recognizing and extracting text from images, such as scanned documents or street signs.

Applications of Computer Vision:

- **Self-Driving Cars**: Autonomous vehicles use computer vision to detect and understand their surroundings, identifying pedestrians, other vehicles, traffic signs, and road conditions.

- **Medical Imaging**: In healthcare, computer vision is used for tasks like detecting tumors in X-ray or MRI images.

- **Retail**: Computer vision is used for inventory management, quality control, and automated checkout systems.

- **Security**: Surveillance cameras with computer vision systems can detect suspicious activities or recognize faces in real-time.

- **Agriculture**: Drones and cameras equipped with computer vision can help in monitoring crops, detecting diseases, and assessing growth.

Computer vision is revolutionizing industries by enabling automation, enhancing accuracy, and providing new capabilities in fields ranging from autonomous driving to healthcare.

10.2 Image Preprocessing: Techniques Like Resizing, Normalization, and Augmentation

Before feeding images into machine learning or deep learning models, we often need to preprocess them. Image preprocessing involves transforming raw images into a format suitable for training. Here are some common preprocessing techniques:

1. Resizing:

Images in datasets often have varying dimensions, and neural networks typically require consistent input sizes. Resizing images to a fixed size ensures that all images are uniform and can be fed into the network.

python

```python
from tensorflow.keras.preprocessing.image import
load_img, img_to_array
```

```
# Load and resize the image
image = load_img('image.jpg', target_size=(64,
64))
image_array = img_to_array(image)
```

2. Normalization:

Normalization is the process of scaling pixel values to a standard range. Since pixel values in an image typically range from 0 to 255, we normalize them by dividing by 255, so they fall between 0 and 1.

python

```
# Normalize the image
image_array = image_array / 255.0
```

Normalization helps the model learn faster and converge more effectively.

3. Data Augmentation:

Data augmentation artificially increases the size of the training dataset by applying random transformations to the images. This technique improves the model's generalization capabilities and prevents overfitting. Common augmentations include rotations, flips, zoom, and shifts.

```python
from tensorflow.keras.preprocessing.image import
ImageDataGenerator

# Create an ImageDataGenerator for data
augmentation
datagen = ImageDataGenerator(
    rotation_range=30,
    width_shift_range=0.2,
    height_shift_range=0.2,
    shear_range=0.2,
    zoom_range=0.2,
    horizontal_flip=True
)

# Apply augmentation to an image
augmented_image                              =
datagen.random_transform(image_array)
```

Why Image Preprocessing is Important:

- It ensures the images are in a suitable format for training neural networks.
- Helps improve the model's performance by reducing overfitting and ensuring consistency.
- Augmentation introduces variability into the training data, which makes the model more robust to real-world scenarios.

137

10.3 Building an Image Classifier: Using CNNs to Classify Images from a Dataset like CIFAR-10

Convolutional Neural Networks (CNNs) are a class of deep learning models specifically designed for image classification tasks. CNNs work by automatically learning spatial hierarchies of features, making them particularly effective for image-related tasks.

Let's build a simple CNN model using the **CIFAR-10 dataset**, a well-known dataset of 60,000 32x32 color images in 10 classes (e.g., airplane, automobile, bird, cat, etc.).

Step 1: Importing Libraries and Dataset

We begin by importing the necessary libraries and loading the CIFAR-10 dataset.

```python
import tensorflow as tf
from tensorflow.keras.models import Sequential
from tensorflow.keras.layers import Conv2D, MaxPooling2D, Flatten, Dense
from tensorflow.keras.datasets import cifar10

# Load the CIFAR-10 dataset
```

```
(X_train,    y_train),    (X_test,    y_test)    =
cifar10.load_data()
```

```
# Normalize the data
X_train, X_test = X_train / 255.0, X_test / 255.0
```

Step 2: Building the CNN Model

We create a CNN model with the following layers:

- **Convolutional layers** to detect features.
- **Pooling layers** to reduce the spatial dimensions.
- **Fully connected layers** for classification.

python

```
# Build the CNN model
model = Sequential([
    Conv2D(32,    (3,    3),    activation='relu',
input_shape=(32, 32, 3)),  # Convolutional layer
    MaxPooling2D((2, 2)),  # Pooling layer
    Conv2D(64, (3, 3), activation='relu'),    #
Another convolutional layer
    MaxPooling2D((2, 2)),  # Pooling layer
    Flatten(),  # Flatten the 3D outputs to 1D
    Dense(64,  activation='relu'),    #  Fully
connected layer
    Dense(10, activation='softmax')  # Output
layer (10 classes)
])
```

139

```
# Compile the model
model.compile(optimizer='adam',
loss='sparse_categorical_crossentropy',
metrics=['accuracy'])
```

In this model:

- The **Conv2D** layers apply filters to detect low-level features like edges, shapes, and textures.
- The **MaxPooling2D** layers reduce the size of the feature maps, which helps improve computational efficiency and reduces overfitting.
- The **Flatten** layer converts the 2D feature maps into a 1D vector, which is then passed to the fully connected layers.
- The **Dense** layer outputs the class probabilities using the **Softmax** activation function.

Step 3: Training the Model

We can now train the model on the training data.

```python
python
```

```
# Train the model
model.fit(X_train,      y_train,      epochs=5,
batch_size=32, validation_data=(X_test, y_test))
```

140

Step 4: Evaluating the Model

After training, we evaluate the model's performance on the test set.

python

```
# Evaluate the model on the test set
test_loss, test_acc = model.evaluate(X_test, y_test)
print(f"Test accuracy: {test_acc * 100:.2f}%")
```

10.4 Real-World Use Case: Object Detection and Image Segmentation

In real-world computer vision tasks, **object detection** and **image segmentation** are more complex than simple image classification. These tasks involve not just recognizing what objects are in an image but also localizing and segmenting them.

1. Object Detection:

Object detection involves identifying and locating objects within an image. It requires both **classification** (what the object is) and **localization** (where the object is). **YOLO**

141

(You Only Look Once) and **Faster R-CNN** are two popular object detection models.

Example:

- **Self-driving cars** use object detection to identify pedestrians, other vehicles, and traffic signs.

2. Image Segmentation:

Image segmentation divides an image into regions or segments, where each region corresponds to a different object or part of the image. **Semantic segmentation** involves classifying each pixel in an image, while **instance segmentation** also differentiates between separate objects of the same class.

Example:

- **Medical imaging** uses segmentation to detect and delineate tumors in MRI or CT scans.

Example of Object Detection Using a Pretrained Model (YOLO):

Using pretrained models like **YOLO**, you can detect objects in real-time.

```python
python

import cv2
import numpy as np

# Load YOLO model
net = cv2.dnn.readNet("yolov3.weights",
"yolov3.cfg")
layer_names = net.getLayerNames()
output_layers = [layer_names[i - 1] for i in
net.getUnconnectedOutLayers()]

# Load an image
img = cv2.imread("image.jpg")
height, width, channels = img.shape

# Prepare image for YOLO model
blob = cv2.dnn.blobFromImage(img, 0.00392, (416,
416), (0, 0, 0), True, crop=False)
net.setInput(blob)
outs = net.forward(output_layers)

# Process and display detected objects
for out in outs:
    for detection in out:
        scores = detection[5:]
        class_id = np.argmax(scores)
        confidence = scores[class_id]
        if confidence > 0.5:
```

143

```
# Draw bounding box
box    =    detection[0:4]    *
np.array([width, height, width, height])
    x, y, w, h = box.astype("int")
    cv2.rectangle(img, (x, y), (x + w, y
+ h), (0, 255, 0), 2)

cv2.imshow("Image", img)
cv2.waitKey(0)
cv2.destroyAllWindows()
```

In this example:

- We load a pretrained **YOLO** model for object detection.
- We process an image and pass it through the model to identify objects.
- Bounding boxes are drawn around detected objects in the image.

Summary

In this chapter, we:

- Learned about **computer vision** and its real-world applications, such as self-driving cars, medical imaging, and facial recognition.
- Explored common **image preprocessing** techniques like resizing, normalization, and augmentation to prepare images for machine learning models.
- Built a simple **image classification model** using **Convolutional Neural Networks (CNNs)** and trained it on the **CIFAR-10 dataset**.
- Discussed more advanced tasks like **object detection** and **image segmentation**, and provided an example of object detection using the **YOLO** model.

Computer vision enables machines to "see" and interpret the world around them, creating numerous possibilities for automation, analysis, and decision-making in various industries. In the next chapter, we will explore **advanced deep learning techniques** like **transfer learning** and **model optimization** to improve the performance of computer vision models.

CHAPTER 11

REINFORCEMENT LEARNING

FUNDAMENTALS

Reinforcement Learning (RL) is one of the most fascinating areas of machine learning. Unlike supervised learning, where the model is trained on labeled data, and unsupervised learning, where the model seeks hidden patterns, reinforcement learning involves teaching an agent to make decisions by interacting with an environment and receiving feedback in the form of **rewards** or **punishments**. The agent learns from these experiences to maximize cumulative rewards over time.

In this chapter, we will explore the fundamentals of reinforcement learning, key concepts such as agents, environments, actions, rewards, and policies, and we will implement a simple **Q-learning** model, a foundational RL algorithm. We will also look at real-world applications of reinforcement learning in **games**, **robotics**, and **autonomous vehicles**.

11.1 What is Reinforcement Learning? An Overview of Reinforcement Learning and How It Differs from Supervised and Unsupervised Learning

Reinforcement Learning (RL) is a type of machine learning where an agent learns to make decisions by performing actions in an environment to achieve a goal. Unlike supervised learning, where the model learns from labeled data, and unsupervised learning, where the model tries to find patterns in unlabeled data, **reinforcement learning** is driven by **rewards** and **punishments**.

Key Features of Reinforcement Learning:

- **Learning through Interaction**: In RL, an agent interacts with its environment by taking actions and observing the consequences (rewards or punishments). It learns by trial and error.
- **No Explicit Supervision**: Unlike supervised learning, where the correct answer is provided during training, the agent in RL learns from its experiences (feedback).
- **Goal-Oriented**: The agent's goal is to maximize cumulative rewards over time, known as **return**.

Key Differences Between Reinforcement Learning and Other Learning Paradigms:

Feature	Supervised Learning	Unsupervised Learning	Reinforcement Learning
Data Type	Labeled data	Unlabeled data	Feedback from environment (rewards)
Learning Process	Learn a mapping from input to output	Discover patterns and structures	Learn by trial and error, maximize rewards
Goal	Predict output for given inputs	Identify patterns in data	Maximize cumulative reward over time
Examples	Classification, regression	Clustering, anomaly detection	Game playing, robotic control

In RL, the learning process is typically described as a **Markov Decision Process (MDP)**, where the agent learns to choose actions that lead to the best long-term rewards.

11.2 Key Concepts: Agents, Environments, Actions, Rewards, and Policies

Understanding the basic components of reinforcement learning is essential to grasp how it works. Here are the core elements:

1. Agent:

- The **agent** is the decision-maker in the RL system. It interacts with the environment by performing actions and receiving rewards or penalties.
- The agent can be a robot, a software program, or any entity that needs to make decisions to achieve a goal.

2. Environment:

- The **environment** is everything that the agent interacts with. It can be a physical world (e.g., a robot navigating through a maze) or a simulated environment (e.g., a video game or a stock market simulation).
- The environment provides feedback to the agent, usually in the form of a reward or penalty.

3. Actions:

- An **action** is a decision or move the agent makes. The set of all possible actions the agent can take is called the **action space**.
- The agent selects an action based on its current state in the environment.

4. Rewards:

- A **reward** is the feedback the agent receives after taking an action in the environment. It can be positive (indicating a good move) or negative (indicating a bad move).
- The agent's goal is to maximize the cumulative reward over time, which encourages it to learn which actions lead to positive outcomes.

5. Policies:

- A **policy** is a strategy or mapping from states to actions. It determines the agent's behavior by specifying which action to take in each state of the environment.
- The goal of reinforcement learning is to learn an optimal policy that maximizes the long-term reward.

6. Value Function:

- The **value function** estimates the expected return (future rewards) for each state or state-action pair. It helps the agent decide the best actions to take.

11.3 Building a Reinforcement Learning Model: A Simple Q-Learning Implementation for an Agent to Navigate a Grid

One of the simplest RL algorithms is **Q-learning**, which is used to learn the value of actions in different states, allowing an agent to make decisions that maximize cumulative rewards. The key concept behind Q-learning is the **Q-table**, which stores the expected future rewards for each state-action pair.

In this example, we'll implement a simple Q-learning model where the agent navigates through a grid to reach a goal while avoiding obstacles. The agent will receive positive rewards for reaching the goal and negative rewards for hitting obstacles.

Step 1: Define the Environment

Let's create a simple environment where an agent moves in a 5x5 grid. The agent starts at a random position, and the goal is to reach the bottom-right corner of the grid.

```python
import numpy as np
import random

# Define the grid environment
grid_size = 5
goal = (4, 4)   # Goal is at the bottom-right corner
obstacles = [(2, 2), (1, 3)]   # Positions of obstacles

# Define actions
actions = ['up', 'down', 'left', 'right']

# Initialize Q-table
Q = np.zeros((grid_size, grid_size, len(actions)))

# Reward system
def get_reward(state):
    if state == goal:
```

```
        return 100   # Reward for reaching the
goal
    elif state in obstacles:
        return -100   # Penalty for hitting
obstacles
    else:
        return -1  # Small penalty for each step
to encourage faster completion
```

Step 2: Q-Learning Algorithm

We will define the Q-learning algorithm, where the agent updates its Q-values based on the reward received after each action. The Q-value update rule is:

$Q(s,a)=Q(s,a)+\alpha[r+\gamma\max_a Q(s',a')-Q(s,a)]Q(s, a) = Q(s, a) + \alpha [r + \gamma \max_a Q(s', a') - Q(s, a)]Q(s,a)=Q(s,a)+\alpha[r+\gamma a \max Q(s',a')-Q(s,a)]$

Where:

- α\alpha$\alpha$ is the learning rate.
- γ\gamma$\gamma$ is the discount factor.
- rrr is the reward received after taking action aaa from state sss.
- s'ss' is the new state after taking action aaa.

```
python
```

```python
# Initialize parameters
alpha = 0.1  # Learning rate
gamma = 0.9  # Discount factor
epsilon = 0.1  # Exploration rate


# Define function to choose action (epsilon-
greedy strategy)
def choose_action(state):
    if random.uniform(0, 1) < epsilon:
        return
random.choice(range(len(actions)))                #
Exploration
    else:
        return np.argmax(Q[state[0], state[1]])
# Exploitation (choose best action)


# Define function to move the agent
def move_agent(state, action):
    if actions[action] == 'up':
        return (max(0, state[0] - 1), state[1])
    elif actions[action] == 'down':
        return (min(grid_size - 1, state[0] + 1),
state[1])
    elif actions[action] == 'left':
        return (state[0], max(0, state[1] - 1))
    elif actions[action] == 'right':
        return (state[0], min(grid_size - 1,
state[1] + 1))
```

154

```
# Training the agent
for episode in range(1000):  # Train for 1000
episodes
    state = (0, 0)   # Start from the top-left
corner
    while state != goal:  # Continue until the
agent reaches the goal
        action = choose_action(state)
        next_state = move_agent(state, action)
        reward = get_reward(next_state)

        # Q-value update
        Q[state[0],    state[1],    action]    =
Q[state[0], state[1], action] + alpha * (reward
+      gamma      *       np.max(Q[next_state[0],
next_state[1]]) - Q[state[0], state[1], action])

        state = next_state  # Move to the next
state
```

Step 3: Evaluating the Agent

After training the agent, we can evaluate its learned policy by running the agent from the starting point to see the path it takes.

```
python
```

```
# Evaluate the agent's learned policy
state = (0, 0)
```

155

```
path = [state]
while state != goal:
    action = np.argmax(Q[state[0], state[1]])   #
Exploitation (choose best action)
    state = move_agent(state, action)
    path.append(state)


print("Path to goal:", path)
```

11.4 Real-World Examples: Reinforcement Learning in Games, Robotics, and Autonomous Vehicles

Reinforcement learning has many real-world applications, particularly in areas that require decision-making and learning from experience. Here are some key use cases:

1. Reinforcement Learning in Games

- **AlphaGo**: One of the most famous applications of RL was **AlphaGo**, developed by DeepMind. AlphaGo defeated human champions in the game of **Go**, a game known for its complexity. The RL model learned by playing millions of games against itself, improving over time.
- **Atari Games**: DeepMind's early work in reinforcement learning involved training agents to

play **Atari video games**. The agent learned to play by receiving pixel-based input and reward signals based on the score, using RL techniques like **Q-learning**.

2. Reinforcement Learning in Robotics

- **Robotic Arm Control**: RL is used in robotics for tasks like controlling robotic arms. The robot learns to perform tasks (e.g., picking up objects, assembling parts) by interacting with its environment and receiving feedback from its actions.
- **Robotic Navigation**: Autonomous robots, such as warehouse robots, use RL to navigate complex environments and optimize tasks like pathfinding and object retrieval.

3. Reinforcement Learning in Autonomous Vehicles

- **Self-Driving Cars**: RL is used in autonomous vehicles to make real-time driving decisions. The car learns to navigate by interacting with its environment (e.g., road conditions, pedestrians) and receiving rewards for safe and efficient driving.
- **Traffic Signal Control**: RL can optimize traffic signal timings in real-time to reduce congestion and

improve traffic flow, learning from traffic patterns and adjusting based on the environment.

Summary

In this chapter, we:

- Explored the basics of **reinforcement learning (RL)**, understanding how it differs from supervised and unsupervised learning.
- Discussed key **RL concepts** such as agents, environments, actions, rewards, and policies.
- Built a simple **Q-learning model** to navigate an agent through a grid environment, demonstrating how RL algorithms learn from interaction with the environment.
- Examined real-world applications of RL in **games**, **robotics**, and **autonomous vehicles**, highlighting the power and versatility of reinforcement learning in complex decision-making tasks.

Reinforcement learning has proven to be a powerful tool in environments where decision-making over time is critical. In the next chapter, we will explore **deep reinforcement**

learning, a powerful combination of deep learning and RL techniques that allows agents to learn directly from high-dimensional inputs like images and videos.

CHAPTER 12

BUILDING A RECOMMENDATION

SYSTEM

Recommendation systems are one of the most widely used applications of machine learning and AI. These systems help users discover relevant content, products, or services by providing personalized suggestions. Companies like **Netflix**, **Amazon**, and **Spotify** use recommendation systems to improve user experience by recommending movies, products, or music based on users' preferences.

In this chapter, we will introduce the fundamental concepts behind recommendation systems, such as **collaborative filtering**, **content-based filtering**, and **hybrid models**. We will also build a simple recommendation engine from scratch using Python.

12.1 What is a Recommendation System? Introduction to Recommendation Systems Used by Platforms Like Netflix and Amazon

A **recommendation system** (or recommender system) is a type of machine learning algorithm used to predict the most relevant items for a user. These systems are commonly found in platforms like:

- **Netflix**: Recommending movies or TV shows based on your viewing history and preferences.
- **Amazon**: Suggesting products based on previous purchases and browsing activity.
- **Spotify**: Recommending music based on your listening habits and preferences.

Recommendation systems enhance user experience by providing personalized content tailored to individual preferences, which increases user engagement and satisfaction.

Key Types of Recommendation Systems:

1. **Collaborative Filtering**: Recommends items based on the interactions between users and items. It

leverages past user behavior to find patterns and similarities between users.

2. **Content-Based Filtering**: Recommends items based on the attributes of the items themselves (e.g., genre, category, features).

3. **Hybrid Models**: Combine both collaborative and content-based filtering to improve recommendation quality.

12.2 Collaborative Filtering: Using User-Item Interactions to Make Recommendations

Collaborative filtering is one of the most popular techniques for building recommendation systems. It recommends items based on the preferences or behaviors of similar users. Collaborative filtering is divided into two types:

1. **User-based Collaborative Filtering**: Recommends items by finding users who are similar to the target user (based on their past interactions) and recommending items that these similar users liked.

2. **Item-based Collaborative Filtering**: Recommends items that are similar to the items the user has liked or interacted with in the past.

How Collaborative Filtering Works:

- **Similarity Matrix**: A matrix is created to capture interactions between users and items. This matrix can be sparse (with many missing values), and the goal is to fill in the missing values by calculating similarities between users or items.
- **Cosine Similarity**: One common way to calculate similarity between users or items is through **cosine similarity**, which measures the angle between two vectors in a multidimensional space.

Example: User-Item Interaction Matrix

Consider the following matrix, where rows represent users and columns represent movies. The values indicate whether a user has watched a movie (1 for watched, 0 for not watched):

User/Movies	Movie A	Movie B	Movie C	Movie D	Movie E
User 1	1	0	1	0	0
User 2	1	1	0	1	0
User 3	0	1	1	1	0
User 4	0	0	1	1	1

By calculating similarities between users or items, we can predict whether a user might enjoy a particular movie.

12.3 Content-Based Filtering: Making Recommendations Based on Item Characteristics

Content-based filtering recommends items by comparing the features or attributes of items to the user's preferences. Unlike collaborative filtering, which relies on user behavior, content-based filtering focuses on the properties of the items themselves.

How Content-Based Filtering Works:

- **Item Features**: Items are represented by their features (e.g., genre, director, actors for movies, or

164

product specifications for items). The system learns which features the user prefers.

- **User Profile**: A user profile is built based on the user's interactions with items, capturing the features of the items the user has shown interest in.

- **Similarity Measure**: The system recommends items that are similar to those the user has interacted with, based on features like content, tags, and descriptions.

Example:

If a user has watched and liked several **action** movies, the recommendation system may suggest other **action** movies, taking into account additional features like actors, directors, or movie ratings.

12.4 Hybrid Models: Combining Collaborative and Content-Based Filtering

Hybrid models combine multiple recommendation techniques to improve the quality and accuracy of recommendations. By combining **collaborative filtering** and **content-based filtering**, hybrid models take advantage of the strengths of both methods, overcoming the limitations of each.

Types of Hybrid Models:

1. **Weighted Hybrid**: The predictions of both methods are combined, and the results are weighted based on the accuracy of each method.

2. **Switching Hybrid**: The system switches between collaborative filtering and content-based filtering depending on the situation (e.g., use content-based when the user has limited data and collaborative filtering when sufficient user-item interactions exist).

3. **Mixed Hybrid**: Combines multiple recommendations into one, providing a list of items recommended by both methods.

4. **Cascade Hybrid**: One model (e.g., collaborative filtering) is used first to generate candidate recommendations, which are then ranked or filtered by another model (e.g., content-based filtering).

Hybrid models are commonly used in real-world applications like **Netflix** and **Amazon** to provide the best of both worlds and handle various scenarios effectively.

12.5 Building a Simple Recommender: Hands-On Project Building a Basic Recommendation Engine

Let's now build a simple recommendation system using **Collaborative Filtering** (with **cosine similarity**) and **Content-Based Filtering**. We'll use a small dataset of movies and user ratings for this example.

Step 1: Import Libraries and Dataset

python

```
import pandas as pd
import numpy as np
from       sklearn.metrics.pairwise       import
cosine_similarity

# Example  dataset  of  user-item  interactions
(ratings of movies)
data = {'User': ['User 1', 'User 2', 'User 3',
'User 4'],
        'Movie A': [5, 3, 0, 1],
        'Movie B': [4, 0, 0, 1],
        'Movie C': [1, 1, 0, 5],
        'Movie D': [0, 1, 5, 4],
        'Movie E': [1, 0, 5, 4]}

df = pd.DataFrame(data)
```

```
df.set_index('User', inplace=True)
```

Step 2: Collaborative Filtering using Cosine Similarity

```
python
```

```python
# Calculate cosine similarity between users
user_similarity = cosine_similarity(df)
user_similarity_df                          =
pd.DataFrame(user_similarity,    index=df.index,
columns=df.index)

# Display the similarity matrix
print(user_similarity_df)
```

Step 3: Content-Based Filtering Example

For content-based filtering, we'll use a simple movie attribute dataset:

```
python
```

```python
# Example content-based features (genres)
movie_features    =    {'Movie    A':    ['Action',
'Thriller'],
                 'Movie      B':      ['Drama',
'Romance'],
                 'Movie      C':      ['Action',
'Comedy'],
                 'Movie      D':      ['Comedy',
'Drama'],
```

```
                    'Movie   E':   ['Action',   'Sci-
Fi']}

# Convert movie features to a DataFrame
features_df = pd.DataFrame(movie_features).T

# Calculate cosine similarity between movies
based on their genres
movie_similarity                              =
cosine_similarity(features_df, features_df)
movie_similarity_df                           =
pd.DataFrame(movie_similarity,
index=features_df.index,
columns=features_df.index)

# Display the similarity between movies based on
content
print(movie_similarity_df)
```

Step 4: Making Recommendations

We can now use the collaborative filtering and content-based filtering results to recommend movies to users. Here's an example where we recommend movies to **User 1** based on collaborative filtering and movie similarity based on content:

```
python
```

```
# Collaborative filtering recommendation for User
1
user_1_similar_users = user_similarity_df['User
1'].sort_values(ascending=False)
print("Collaborative Filtering Recommendations
for User 1:")
print(user_1_similar_users)

# Content-based recommendation based on
similarity to Movie A
similar_movies_to_A = movie_similarity_df['Movie
A'].sort_values(ascending=False)
print("\nContent-Based Recommendations for Movie
A:")
print(similar_movies_to_A)
```

Summary

In this chapter, we:

- Introduced **recommendation systems** and explored how platforms like **Netflix** and **Amazon** use them to enhance user experience by providing personalized suggestions.
- Learned about **Collaborative Filtering** and **Content-Based Filtering**, two key techniques used in recommendation systems.

- Built a simple recommender system combining both approaches, demonstrating the use of **cosine similarity** for both user-item interactions and item characteristics.

- Explored **hybrid models**, which combine multiple recommendation techniques to improve accuracy and flexibility.

Recommendation systems are powerful tools for personalizing user experiences, and their applications are widespread in industries ranging from e-commerce to entertainment. In the next chapter, we will delve into **evaluation metrics** for recommendation systems, helping you understand how to assess their effectiveness and performance.

CHAPTER 13

WORKING WITH AI APIS AND TOOLS

Artificial Intelligence (AI) has rapidly transformed from a field of research into a set of practical tools that businesses and developers can use to create powerful applications. One of the easiest and most efficient ways to integrate AI capabilities into your applications is by using **prebuilt AI tools** and **APIs** provided by major cloud providers like **Google Cloud**, **Amazon Web Services (AWS)**, and **Microsoft Azure**. These APIs provide access to pre-trained models, allowing you to integrate complex AI tasks such as image recognition, natural language processing (NLP), and more, without needing to build and train models from scratch.

In this chapter, we will explore AI APIs and pre-trained models offered by cloud providers, show how to integrate these tools into your application, and walk through an example of building an AI app with these APIs.

13.1 Prebuilt AI Tools: Overview of AI APIs and Pre-trained Models from Providers Like Google Cloud, AWS, and Microsoft Azure

Major cloud providers offer a variety of **AI services** that cover different aspects of artificial intelligence, including machine learning, computer vision, NLP, and speech recognition. These services give developers access to powerful AI models through simple API calls, removing the complexity of training and tuning models.

1. Google Cloud AI

Google Cloud provides a wide range of AI and machine learning APIs through its **Cloud AI Platform**. Some popular services include:

- **Vision AI**: Offers image recognition capabilities such as label detection, object detection, and text extraction from images.
- **Cloud Natural Language API**: Performs sentiment analysis, entity recognition, and text classification.
- **Dialogflow**: A platform for building conversational interfaces, such as chatbots and virtual assistants.

173

- **Translation API**: Detects language and translates text to other languages.

2. AWS AI Services

Amazon Web Services (AWS) provides a suite of machine learning and AI services under its **AI and ML** offering. Some notable services are:

- **Amazon Rekognition**: Provides powerful image and video analysis tools for detecting objects, faces, and activities in media.
- **Amazon Comprehend**: Natural language processing tools for sentiment analysis, entity recognition, and text summarization.
- **Amazon Polly**: Converts text into lifelike speech, useful for building voice-enabled applications.
- **Amazon Lex**: A service for building conversational agents (chatbots), integrated with AWS Lambda for backend logic.

3. Microsoft Azure AI

Microsoft Azure offers a variety of AI services under **Azure Cognitive Services**, enabling developers to add AI capabilities to their applications with ease. Key services include:

- **Computer Vision API**: Analyzes images and videos to identify objects, extract text, and recognize scenes.
- **Text Analytics API**: Provides sentiment analysis, language detection, and key phrase extraction.
- **Azure Bot Service**: Used for creating conversational bots that can be deployed across multiple channels.
- **Speech Services**: Converts speech to text, text to speech, and enables speech translation.

These APIs are highly optimized and can be integrated easily with existing applications to enable powerful AI functionalities, all without the need for specialized machine learning knowledge.

13.2 Using Pre-trained Models: How to Integrate AI Tools Like Image Recognition and NLP into Your Application Without Building Models from Scratch

Integrating **pre-trained models** from AI providers is one of the most efficient ways to add machine learning functionality to your app. These models have already been trained on massive datasets and are available for use via simple API calls.

Example 1: Image Recognition with Google Cloud Vision API

The **Google Cloud Vision API** allows you to integrate image recognition capabilities into your app. It can recognize objects, faces, and even read text from images using Optical Character Recognition (OCR).

To use the Vision API, you would need to:

1. Sign up for a Google Cloud account and enable the Vision API.
2. Install the Google Cloud client library.
3. Call the API to process images and get results.

Example Python code to detect labels in an image:

```python
from google.cloud import vision
import io

# Initialize the Vision API client
client = vision.ImageAnnotatorClient()

# Load image
```

```
with io.open('image.jpg', 'rb') as image_file:
    content = image_file.read()

image = vision.Image(content=content)

# Perform label detection
response = client.label_detection(image=image)
labels = response.label_annotations

# Print detected labels
for label in labels:
    print(f"Label: {label.description}, Score:
{label.score}")
```

This code uploads an image to the Google Cloud Vision API and retrieves the labels (e.g., objects or categories) detected in the image. No deep learning model training is required—simply upload the image and receive the results.

Example 2: Text Classification with AWS Comprehend

AWS **Comprehend** provides natural language processing (NLP) capabilities like sentiment analysis, language detection, and entity recognition. You can integrate text analysis into your app with just a few lines of code.

Example Python code to perform sentiment analysis:

```python

import boto3

# Initialize the AWS Comprehend client
comprehend = boto3.client(service_name='comprehend', region_name='us-east-1')

# Text to analyze
text = "I love working with machine learning!"

# Call AWS Comprehend's sentiment analysis API
response = comprehend.detect_sentiment(Text=text, LanguageCode='en')

# Print the sentiment
print(f"Sentiment: {response['Sentiment']}")
```

This code sends a sentence to AWS Comprehend and retrieves the sentiment of the text (positive, negative, neutral, or mixed). It's a simple way to add sentiment analysis capabilities to your app.

Example 3: Speech-to-Text with Microsoft Azure Speech Services

Microsoft **Azure Speech Services** enables converting speech to text. It can be used to transcribe audio from conversations, lectures, or interviews.

Example Python code to transcribe speech:

```python
python

import azure.cognitiveservices.speech as speechsdk

# Create a speech configuration instance using your API key and region
speech_config = speechsdk.SpeechConfig(subscription="YOUR_API_K
EY", region="YOUR_REGION")

# Create a speech recognizer instance
speech_recognizer = speechsdk.SpeechRecognizer(speech_config=speech
_config)

# Start speech recognition from an audio file
result = speech_recognizer.recognize_once_from_file("aud
io.wav")
```

```
# Print the transcribed text
print(f"Recognized text: {result.text}")
```

In this example, Azure's Speech-to-Text service transcribes an audio file into text. This is a great feature for creating applications that require voice-based input.

13.3 Building an AI App with APIs: Example of Using AI APIs for Building a Chatbot or an Image Classification App

Now, let's combine the power of AI APIs to build a simple application. We'll create a **chatbot** using **Dialogflow** (from Google Cloud) and **Image Classification** using the **Google Cloud Vision API**.

1. Building a Chatbot with Dialogflow API

Dialogflow is a Google Cloud service for building conversational agents, like chatbots. It allows users to create bots that can handle user queries, respond intelligently, and integrate with various platforms (e.g., websites, Slack, Facebook Messenger).

Steps to build a basic chatbot:

1. Sign up for **Dialogflow** and create a new agent.
2. Define intents (specific user queries) and provide responses.
3. Use the **Dialogflow API** to interact with the chatbot.

```python
import dialogflow_v2 as dialogflow

# Set up authentication and project information
project_id = 'your-project-id'
session_id = 'your-session-id'
language_code = 'en'

# Initialize the Dialogflow session client
session_client = dialogflow.SessionsClient()
session                                      =
session_client.session_path(project_id,
session_id)

# Create a text input for the user query
text_input                                   =
dialogflow.types.TextInput(text='What    is    the
weather today?', language_code=language_code)
query_input                                  =
dialogflow.types.QueryInput(text=text_input)

# Detect intent from the user's query
```

181

```
response                                =
session_client.detect_intent(session=session,
query_input=query_input)

# Print the response from the chatbot
print(f"Query                           text:
{response.query_result.query_text}")
print(f"Response:
{response.query_result.fulfillment_text}")
```

In this example, the chatbot responds to a user query about the weather, showing how easily you can integrate Dialogflow into your app.

2. Building an Image Classification App

You can combine the **Google Cloud Vision API** with the chatbot to build a complete app. For example, the app could allow users to upload an image and ask questions about the content of the image, with the chatbot providing answers based on the image's features.

```
python
```

```
# Assuming we have a chatbot object and image
uploading system in place
image_path = 'image.jpg'
```

```
# Call the Vision API to classify the image
image = vision.Image(filename=image_path)
response = client.label_detection(image=image)

# Process the response to give the chatbot
context about the image
labels = [label.description for label in
response.label_annotations]
labels_string = ', '.join(labels)

# Respond with information about the image
response = chatbot.ask(f"What is in this image?
It contains: {labels_string}")
```

In this case, the chatbot can provide responses based on both the textual queries and the image content, creating a multimodal AI system.

Summary

In this chapter, we:

- Explored the concept of **AI APIs** and pre-trained models from major providers like **Google Cloud**, **AWS**, and **Microsoft Azure**, which allow developers to quickly integrate AI capabilities into their applications.

- Learned how to use **pre-trained models** for tasks like image recognition, sentiment analysis, and speech-to-text without building models from scratch.
- Built a simple application using AI APIs, including creating a **chatbot** with **Dialogflow** and integrating the **Google Cloud Vision API** for image classification.

AI APIs significantly simplify the development process and provide powerful tools for building intelligent applications. In the next chapter, we will explore **AI model deployment** techniques, discussing how to deploy models to the cloud, on mobile devices, and edge devices for production use.

CHAPTER 14

MODEL EVALUATION AND HYPERPARAMETER TUNING

Building a machine learning or deep learning model is only part of the process—ensuring that the model performs optimally in real-world scenarios is equally important. **Model evaluation** helps us understand how well a model generalizes to unseen data, and **hyperparameter tuning** allows us to optimize the model for better performance. In this chapter, we will cover techniques for **evaluating model performance**, and discuss **hyperparameter tuning** methods such as **grid search** and **random search**. Finally, we'll walk through practical examples of **hyperparameter tuning** to build more accurate and efficient models.

14.1 Evaluating Model Performance: Methods for Assessing Model Accuracy, Including Cross-Validation

Evaluating a model's performance is essential to understand how well it generalizes to new data. A model may perform well on the training data but fail to generalize to unseen data, which is known as **overfitting**. Evaluating the model helps identify this issue and select the best model for deployment.

1. Split the Data into Training and Testing Sets

The most basic way to evaluate a model is by splitting the data into **training** and **testing** sets. Typically, the training set is used to train the model, and the testing set is used to evaluate its performance. A common split ratio is **80/20** or **70/30**, where 80% (or 70%) of the data is used for training and the remaining 20% (or 30%) is reserved for testing.

python

```
from sklearn.model_selection import train_test_split

# Example dataset (X = features, y = target)
X_train, X_test, y_train, y_test = train_test_split(X, y, test_size=0.2, random_state=42)
```

2. Cross-Validation

Cross-validation is a more robust technique for evaluating model performance. It involves splitting the data into multiple folds (typically 5 or 10), training the model on some folds, and testing it on the remaining fold. This process is repeated for each fold, and the performance is averaged to provide a more reliable estimate of the model's accuracy.

The most common type of cross-validation is **k-fold cross-validation**. For example, with 5-fold cross-validation, the data is split into 5 parts, and the model is trained and tested 5 times, each time using a different fold as the testing set.

python

```
from        sklearn.model_selection        import
cross_val_score
from          sklearn.ensemble          import
RandomForestClassifier

# Example model: Random Forest Classifier
model = RandomForestClassifier()

# Perform 5-fold cross-validation
scores = cross_val_score(model, X, y, cv=5)
print(f"Cross-validation scores: {scores}")
print(f"Mean accuracy: {scores.mean()}")
```

187

Cross-validation provides a more reliable estimate of the model's generalization performance by reducing the variance associated with a single train-test split.

3. Performance Metrics

Evaluating model performance also requires selecting appropriate metrics. Common evaluation metrics include:

- **Accuracy**: The percentage of correct predictions out of all predictions.

  Accuracy=Number of Correct PredictionsTotal Number of Predictions\text{Accuracy} = \frac{\text{Number of Correct Predictions}}{\text{Total Number of Predictions}}Accuracy=Total Number of PredictionsNumber of Correct Predictions

- **Precision**: The proportion of true positive predictions among all positive predictions.

  Precision=TPTP+FP\text{Precision} = \frac{TP}{TP + FP}Precision=TP+FPTP

- **Recall**: The proportion of true positive predictions among all actual positives.

Recall=TPTP+FN\text{Recall} = \frac{TP}{TP + FN}Recall=TP+FNTP

- **F1-Score**: The harmonic mean of precision and recall.

F1=2×Precision×RecallPrecision+RecallF1 = 2 \times \frac{\text{Precision} \times \text{Recall}}{\text{Precision} + \text{Recall}}F1=2×Precision+RecallPrecision×Recall

- **ROC and AUC**: For binary classification, the **Receiver Operating Characteristic (ROC)** curve and **Area Under the Curve (AUC)** are used to evaluate model performance across different classification thresholds.

```python
from sklearn.metrics import accuracy_score, classification_report

# Evaluate the model
y_pred = model.predict(X_test)
print(f"Accuracy: {accuracy_score(y_test, y_pred)}")
print(classification_report(y_test, y_pred))
```

189

The choice of metric depends on the problem at hand. For example, **precision** and **recall** are more useful in imbalanced classification problems, while **accuracy** is typically used when classes are balanced.

14.2 Hyperparameter Tuning: Techniques Like Grid Search and Random Search for Optimizing Model Parameters

Hyperparameter tuning refers to the process of selecting the best hyperparameters for a model to maximize its performance. Hyperparameters are the parameters set before training the model, and they affect the model's learning process.

1. Grid Search

Grid search is an exhaustive search method where all possible combinations of hyperparameters are tested to find the best one. The main drawback of grid search is that it can be computationally expensive, especially for large datasets and many hyperparameters.

Example of performing a grid search to tune hyperparameters for a **Random Forest Classifier**:

```python
python

from sklearn.model_selection import GridSearchCV
from sklearn.ensemble import RandomForestClassifier

# Define the model
model = RandomForestClassifier()

# Define the hyperparameter grid
param_grid = {
    'n_estimators': [50, 100, 200],
    'max_depth': [10, 20, None],
    'min_samples_split': [2, 5, 10]
}

# Perform grid search with 5-fold cross-validation
grid_search = GridSearchCV(estimator=model, param_grid=param_grid, cv=5)
grid_search.fit(X_train, y_train)

# Print the best hyperparameters
print(f"Best hyperparameters: {grid_search.best_params_}")
```

In this example:

- We define a grid of possible values for the hyperparameters (`n_estimators`, `max_depth`, and `min_samples_split`).
- The `GridSearchCV` function will evaluate all possible combinations of these hyperparameters and return the best-performing set.

2. Random Search

Random search is another approach where random combinations of hyperparameters are tested. While it does not explore the entire hyperparameter space as exhaustively as grid search, it often performs better in a shorter amount of time, especially when there are many hyperparameters.

Example of performing random search for a **Random Forest Classifier**:

python

```
from       sklearn.model_selection       import
RandomizedSearchCV
from scipy.stats import randint

# Define the model
model = RandomForestClassifier()
```

```
# Define the hyperparameter distribution
param_dist = {
    'n_estimators': randint(50, 200),
    'max_depth': [None, 10, 20, 30],
    'min_samples_split': randint(2, 10)
}

# Perform random search with 5-fold cross-
validation
random_search                            =
RandomizedSearchCV(estimator=model,
param_distributions=param_dist, n_iter=10, cv=5)
random_search.fit(X_train, y_train)

# Print the best hyperparameters
print(f"Best                hyperparameters:
{random_search.best_params_}")
```

In this example:

- We define a distribution for the hyperparameters and perform random search with 10 random combinations of these values.
- RandomizedSearchCV is less computationally expensive than grid search and is useful when dealing with a large number of hyperparameters.

3. Bayesian Optimization and Other Techniques

- **Bayesian optimization** is another hyperparameter tuning technique that uses probability models to efficiently search the hyperparameter space. It balances exploration and exploitation, allowing it to find good hyperparameters faster than grid search or random search.
- Other methods like **genetic algorithms** and **gradient-based optimization** are also used for hyperparameter tuning, depending on the complexity and type of model.

14.3 Building an Optimized Model: Practical Examples of Tuning Hyperparameters for Machine Learning and Deep Learning Models

Let's apply hyperparameter tuning to a deep learning model, such as a **Convolutional Neural Network (CNN)**, to classify images from the **CIFAR-10 dataset**.

Step 1: Define the CNN Model

python

```
from tensorflow.keras.models import Sequential
```

```python
from tensorflow.keras.layers import Conv2D,
MaxPooling2D, Flatten, Dense
from tensorflow.keras.datasets import cifar10
from tensorflow.keras.optimizers import Adam

# Load the CIFAR-10 dataset
(X_train, y_train), (X_test, y_test) =
cifar10.load_data()
X_train, X_test = X_train / 255.0, X_test / 255.0

# Define the CNN model
def create_model(learning_rate=0.001,
filters=32, kernel_size=(3, 3)):
    model = Sequential([
        Conv2D(filters, kernel_size,
activation='relu', input_shape=(32, 32, 3)),
        MaxPooling2D(pool_size=(2, 2)),
        Conv2D(filters*2, kernel_size,
activation='relu'),
        MaxPooling2D(pool_size=(2, 2)),
        Flatten(),
        Dense(64, activation='relu'),
        Dense(10, activation='softmax')
    ])

model.compile(optimizer=Adam(learning_rate=lear
ning_rate),
loss='sparse_categorical_crossentropy',
metrics=['accuracy'])
```

```
return model
```

Step 2: Hyperparameter Tuning with Random Search

Now, let's perform **random search** to optimize the hyperparameters such as the learning rate, number of filters, and kernel size.

```python
python

from        sklearn.model_selection        import
RandomizedSearchCV
from        tensorflow.keras.wrappers.scikit_learn
import KerasClassifier

# Wrap the model as a KerasClassifier for
RandomizedSearchCV
model = KerasClassifier(build_fn=create_model,
epochs=5, batch_size=32, verbose=0)

# Define the hyperparameter space
param_dist = {
    'learning_rate': [0.0001, 0.001, 0.01],
    'filters': [32, 64, 128],
    'kernel_size': [(3, 3), (5, 5)]
}

# Perform random search
```

```
random_search                                    =
RandomizedSearchCV(estimator=model,
param_distributions=param_dist, n_iter=5, cv=3)
random_search.fit(X_train, y_train)

# Print the best hyperparameters
print(f"Best                    hyperparameters:
{random_search.best_params_}")
```

In this example:

- We define a **CNN model** with tunable parameters (learning rate, filters, kernel size).
- We use **random search** to find the best combination of these parameters, optimizing the model's performance.

Summary

In this chapter, we:

- Explored **model evaluation** techniques, including **cross-validation** and performance metrics like accuracy, precision, recall, and F1-score.

- Learned about **hyperparameter tuning** and how to optimize a model's performance using techniques like **grid search** and **random search**.
- Built a deep learning model and applied **hyperparameter tuning** to improve the model's accuracy and efficiency.

Hyperparameter tuning is a crucial step in developing high-performing machine learning and deep learning models. In the next chapter, we will explore **advanced model deployment** techniques, showing how to deploy models to production and use them in real-world applications.

CHAPTER 15

SCALING AI PROJECTS

As artificial intelligence (AI) projects grow in complexity, they require advanced techniques to handle large datasets, computationally intensive models, and ever-increasing demands for performance. **Scalability** in AI refers to the ability to efficiently scale AI systems to manage larger datasets, more complex models, and more users. In this chapter, we will explore the different aspects of scaling AI projects, including the use of cloud-based AI platforms, distributed training techniques, and best practices for deploying AI models into production environments.

15.1 Scalability in AI: How to Scale Your AI Projects to Handle Large Datasets and Complex Models

Scalability is one of the primary challenges in AI development. As the scope of your AI projects expands, you need to ensure that the infrastructure and techniques you use

199

can handle the growing computational load and data storage requirements.

Key Considerations for Scaling AI:

1. **Data Storage and Management**:
   - o **Big Data**: AI models, particularly deep learning models, often require massive amounts of data to train effectively. Storing and managing large datasets efficiently is a crucial consideration. Cloud storage solutions, such as **Google Cloud Storage**, **Amazon S3**, and **Azure Blob Storage**, provide scalable storage for big data.
   - o **Data Pipelines**: Building robust data pipelines ensures that data can be collected, cleaned, preprocessed, and fed into AI models efficiently. Technologies like **Apache Kafka** and **Apache Spark** help manage real-time data streams and large-scale data processing.

2. **Model Complexity**:
   - o Complex models, such as deep neural networks, require significant computational resources, especially during training. As

model complexity increases, so do the demands on **memory**, **CPU/GPU**, and **disk I/O**. For this reason, model architecture and parameter tuning must be optimized to avoid unnecessary overhead.

- For instance, advanced architectures like **Transformer networks** (e.g., BERT, GPT) require large computational resources during both training and inference.

3. **Handling Large Datasets**:

- **Batch Processing**: For training models on large datasets, using batch processing techniques ensures that the model doesn't run out of memory. You can feed the data into the model in smaller chunks (batches) and process the batches sequentially.

- **Data Sharding**: In situations where datasets are too large to fit into memory, **sharding** can be used to divide the data into smaller, manageable pieces and process them in parallel.

4. **Efficient Data Storage Formats**:

- Storing data in optimized formats (e.g., **Parquet** for tabular data, **TFRecord** for

201

TensorFlow, **HDF5** for hierarchical data) helps improve I/O performance and reduces disk space usage when training models on large datasets.

15.2 Cloud AI Platforms: Using Cloud-Based AI Platforms (Google Cloud AI, AWS, etc.) to Deploy and Scale Models

Cloud platforms provide on-demand computing resources that allow you to scale AI models and projects without the need to invest in costly hardware infrastructure. Major cloud providers offer comprehensive services for training, deploying, and scaling AI models.

1. Google Cloud AI:

Google Cloud provides various AI and machine learning services through its **AI Platform**, which includes tools for model training, serving, and scaling:

- **AI Platform Training**: A fully managed service for training machine learning models, including deep learning models, using TensorFlow, PyTorch, and other frameworks. It supports distributed training and hyperparameter tuning.

- **AI Platform Prediction**: For deploying models to production and serving predictions at scale. It supports batch and online prediction, and you can scale the number of instances based on traffic.

- **BigQuery**: A fully managed data warehouse for analyzing large datasets. BigQuery can be used in conjunction with AI Platform to process data at scale.

2. AWS AI Services:

Amazon Web Services (AWS) provides a suite of AI services through its **AWS AI and ML** offerings:

- **Amazon SageMaker**: A managed service for building, training, and deploying machine learning models. SageMaker supports distributed training on **EC2 instances** and **GPU-based instances** for deep learning.

- **AWS Lambda**: For deploying machine learning models as serverless functions. Lambda automatically scales based on incoming requests, making it ideal for infrequent prediction tasks.

- **AWS EC2**: Elastic Compute Cloud (EC2) provides flexible compute resources, including instances equipped with **NVIDIA GPUs** for training complex models like deep neural networks.

3. Microsoft Azure AI:

Microsoft Azure offers a variety of tools for building and scaling AI projects:

- **Azure Machine Learning**: A cloud service that allows you to build, train, and deploy machine learning models. It supports **distributed training** on Azure **GPU** and **CPU** instances and provides an easy-to-use interface for managing model pipelines.
- **Azure Cognitive Services**: Pre-built APIs for adding AI capabilities like image recognition, language understanding, and speech processing to your applications. These APIs are scalable and can be integrated into applications with minimal setup.

Benefits of Cloud AI Platforms:

- **On-demand resources**: Scale computing power up or down depending on your needs, reducing costs.

- **Distributed Training**: Cloud platforms enable the use of distributed systems to train large models across multiple machines or GPUs.

- **Managed Services**: Many cloud platforms offer managed services that automate many aspects of model training and deployment, reducing the complexity for developers.

- **Scalable Storage**: Cloud providers offer scalable storage solutions that grow with your data, making it easy to store and access large datasets.

15.3 Distributed Training: Techniques for Training AI Models on Multiple Machines or GPUs

Distributed training involves splitting the training workload across multiple machines or GPUs to speed up the process and handle large datasets. As AI models, especially deep learning models, grow in complexity, training on a single machine may become impractical due to memory and computational limitations.

Techniques for Distributed Training:

1. **Data Parallelism**:

- o In **data parallelism**, the dataset is divided into smaller chunks, and each chunk is processed on a different machine or GPU. Each machine computes gradients based on its subset of the data, and the gradients are averaged to update the model parameters.
- o Example: **TensorFlow Distributed** and **PyTorch Distributed** allow you to distribute training across multiple GPUs or machines using data parallelism.

2. **Model Parallelism**:

- o In **model parallelism**, the model itself is divided into smaller parts, and each part is trained on a different machine or GPU. This is useful for very large models that cannot fit into the memory of a single GPU.
- o Model parallelism is typically used for **multi-GPU training** or distributed deep learning with very large architectures, like **Transformers** (e.g., GPT and BERT).

3. **Parameter Server Architecture**:

- o A **parameter server** is a distributed system that stores the parameters of a model and updates them during training. Multiple workers (machines or GPUs) compute gradients and send them to the parameter server, which aggregates the gradients and updates the model.

4. **Horovod**:

   o **Horovod** is a popular library for distributed deep learning training. It supports data parallelism and works with TensorFlow, Keras, PyTorch, and Apache MXNet. Horovod uses **Ring-AllReduce** to efficiently distribute the gradients across workers.

Example of Distributed Training with Horovod:

python

```python
import horovod.tensorflow as hvd
import tensorflow as tf

# Initialize Horovod
hvd.init()

# Create the model
model = tf.keras.Sequential([
    tf.keras.layers.Dense(128,
activation='relu', input_shape=(784,)),
    tf.keras.layers.Dense(10,
activation='softmax')
```

207

```
])

# Compile the model
model.compile(optimizer=tf.keras.optimizers.Ada
m(),

loss='sparse_categorical_crossentropy',
            metrics=['accuracy'])

# Distribute the training
model.fit(X_train,      y_train,      epochs=10,
batch_size=64,
callbacks=[hvd.callbacks.BroadcastGlobalVariabl
esCallback(0)])
```

In this example, **Horovod** is used to distribute the training across multiple GPUs, allowing the model to scale efficiently during training.

15.4 Deploying AI Models: Steps to Deploy Your AI Models into Production Environments

Once an AI model is trained and evaluated, it needs to be deployed to a production environment where it can serve real-time predictions or process incoming data.

1. Model Export and Serialization:

Before deployment, the model is usually saved or serialized into a format that can be loaded for inference in production. Common formats include:

- **TensorFlow SavedModel**: A TensorFlow-specific format that includes both the model architecture and trained weights.
- **ONNX (Open Neural Network Exchange)**: A format that allows models to be transferred between different frameworks (e.g., TensorFlow to PyTorch).
- **Pickle**: A Python-specific serialization format often used for smaller machine learning models.

```python
# Example of saving a TensorFlow model
model.save('my_model')
```

2. Model Deployment:

There are several ways to deploy AI models:

- **Cloud-Based Deployment**: Deploying models on platforms like **Google Cloud AI**, **AWS SageMaker**, or **Microsoft Azure Machine Learning**. These platforms offer easy-to-use interfaces for deploying models as APIs for real-time inference.

- **Serverless Deployment**: Using **AWS Lambda** or **Google Cloud Functions**, you can deploy machine learning models as serverless functions that automatically scale based on demand.

- **Edge Deployment**: For applications in IoT or mobile devices, you can deploy models on **edge devices** using frameworks like **TensorFlow Lite** or **ONNX Runtime** for efficient, low-latency inference.

3. Model Monitoring and Updating:

Once the model is deployed, it's important to monitor its performance in the production environment:

- **Model Drift**: Track changes in the distribution of input data over time to detect if the model's performance degrades.

- **Logging and Metrics**: Use logging and monitoring tools to track metrics like **accuracy**, **latency**, and **error rates**.

- **Model Retraining**: Periodically retrain the model with new data to keep it up-to-date and accurate.

Summary

In this chapter, we:

- Explored **scalability** in AI, focusing on techniques for handling large datasets, complex models, and the need for high-performance computation.
- Learned how to use **cloud-based AI platforms** like **Google Cloud AI**, **AWS**, and **Microsoft Azure** to scale and deploy AI models without managing infrastructure.
- Discussed **distributed training** techniques such as **data parallelism** and **model parallelism** to scale AI model training across multiple machines or GPUs.
- Walked through the process of **deploying AI models** into production environments, including model export, cloud deployment, and edge deployment.

Scaling AI projects is critical for handling the increasing complexity and volume of data, and cloud-based solutions provide the flexibility and computational resources needed to deploy AI models at scale. In the next chapter, we will dive into **advanced AI applications** such as **reinforcement learning** in real-world environments.

CHAPTER 16

ETHICAL CONSIDERATIONS IN AI

Artificial Intelligence (AI) has immense potential to revolutionize industries and improve lives. However, as AI systems are deployed in more critical applications, it becomes increasingly important to address the ethical challenges that come with them. From biases in AI models to the need for transparency and explainability, there are several ethical concerns that must be considered to ensure AI is developed and used responsibly. This chapter will explore key ethical considerations in AI, including AI bias, transparency and explainability, AI for good, and the ethical frameworks guiding responsible AI development.

16.1 AI Bias: Understanding How Biases in Data Can Affect AI Models and Lead to Unfair or Discriminatory Results

AI models are only as good as the data they are trained on. **Bias in AI** refers to the systematic and unfair discrimination against certain individuals or groups caused by biases present in the training data. Since AI models learn from historical data, they can inadvertently perpetuate or even amplify existing biases present in society.

Types of AI Bias:

1. **Data Bias**:
   - o **Historical Bias**: If the data used to train a model reflects past inequalities or prejudices, the AI model will learn these biases and may perpetuate them. For example, if a hiring algorithm is trained on historical hiring data where a specific demographic was underrepresented, the model might favor candidates from that demographic.
   - o **Sampling Bias**: Occurs when certain groups are underrepresented in the training data. For example, facial recognition systems have been shown to perform poorly on women and

people of color because they were trained predominantly on images of white males.

2. **Algorithmic Bias**:

   o Bias can also arise from the algorithms themselves, even when the training data is relatively unbiased. Some machine learning algorithms might unintentionally favor certain features or decision boundaries, resulting in biased outcomes.

3. **Label Bias**:

   o **Labeling bias** occurs when human annotators introduce bias into the dataset by inconsistently labeling data. For instance, labeling a person's ethnicity in images could be influenced by cultural biases, which would then affect how the model perceives ethnicity.

Consequences of Bias in AI:

- **Discrimination**: AI systems used in hiring, criminal justice, healthcare, and finance could unfairly disadvantage certain groups based on race, gender, or socio-economic status.

- **Reinforcement of Inequalities**: Biases in AI can reinforce societal stereotypes, exacerbating existing inequalities and potentially entrenching discriminatory practices.

Addressing AI Bias:

- **Diverse Data**: Ensuring that training datasets are diverse and representative of all groups is crucial to mitigate bias. For example, in facial recognition, training on a more diverse set of faces can help reduce gender and racial biases.
- **Bias Audits**: Regularly testing AI models for bias and auditing their decisions can help identify and mitigate potential discriminatory impacts before deployment.
- **Fairness Constraints**: Implementing fairness constraints in the model training process can ensure that the model treats different groups equally.

16.2 Transparency and Explainability: Why AI Models Should Be Explainable and Transparent, and How to Achieve That

AI models, particularly deep learning models, are often referred to as **"black boxes"** because they make predictions without providing clear insights into how they arrived at those decisions. **Explainability** and **transparency** are crucial for building trust in AI systems and ensuring that they are used ethically.

Why Explainability and Transparency Matter:

1. **Trust**: Users are more likely to trust AI systems if they can understand why a decision was made. For example, in healthcare, doctors must understand how an AI system arrived at its diagnosis to make informed decisions.

2. **Accountability**: When AI systems make decisions that impact people's lives, such as in lending or criminal justice, it is important to know who or what is responsible for the decisions and whether those decisions were fair and just.

3. **Bias Detection**: Transparency allows for easier detection of biases in AI models. Without

understanding how a model works, it is difficult to identify and correct biased outcomes.

4. **Compliance**: Regulatory frameworks like the **GDPR** (General Data Protection Regulation) require organizations to explain automated decisions made about individuals. Ensuring AI models are explainable is essential for compliance with such laws.

Achieving Explainability:

1. **Model Agnostic Approaches**:
   o **LIME (Local Interpretable Model-agnostic Explanations)**: LIME is a technique that explains the predictions of any black-box model by approximating it with an interpretable model locally around the prediction.
   o **SHAP (SHapley Additive exPlanations)**: SHAP provides a unified measure of feature importance based on **Shapley values**, a concept from cooperative game theory that fairly attributes contributions to each feature in a prediction.

2. **Interpretable Models**:

217

o   Some machine learning models, like **decision trees**, **linear regression**, and **logistic regression**, are inherently more interpretable than complex models like deep neural networks. When interpretability is critical, these simpler models may be preferred.

3. **Visualization**:

o   Visualization tools like **Saliency Maps** and **Grad-CAM** (Gradient-weighted Class Activation Mapping) are used to visualize what parts of an image influenced a model's prediction, making deep learning models more transparent in tasks like image classification.

Example: Using LIME for Model Explainability:

python

```
import lime
from        lime.lime_tabular       import
LimeTabularExplainer

# Assuming you have a trained model and test data
explainer   =   LimeTabularExplainer(X_train,
training_labels=y_train, mode='classification')
```

```
# Pick a test instance to explain
test_instance = X_test.iloc[0]

# Generate an explanation for the instance
explanation                              =
explainer.explain_instance(test_instance,
model.predict_proba)

# Show the explanation
explanation.show_in_notebook()
```

This example uses **LIME** to explain a classification model's prediction for a specific test instance.

16.3 AI for Good: Exploring How AI Can Be Used for Social Good and Solving Global Challenges

AI is not only used for profit-driven goals but can also be harnessed for the greater good, helping address global challenges and improve social welfare. **AI for Good** refers to using AI to solve problems that can positively impact society, ranging from healthcare to climate change.

Examples of AI for Social Good:

1. **Healthcare**:

219

- o **Disease Prediction**: AI models can be used to predict outbreaks of diseases like **Ebola** or **COVID-19** by analyzing patterns in healthcare data and real-time reports.
- o **Medical Imaging**: AI algorithms can assist in diagnosing diseases such as cancer, detecting tumors in X-rays, MRIs, or CT scans with high accuracy.
- o **Drug Discovery**: AI has accelerated drug discovery by predicting which compounds could be effective for treating diseases, dramatically reducing the time needed for research and development.

2. **Climate Change**:
   - o **Climate Modeling**: AI can improve climate predictions and help scientists understand the impacts of climate change by analyzing large datasets related to weather patterns and environmental changes.
   - o **Energy Efficiency**: AI can optimize energy consumption in buildings and industrial processes, helping reduce greenhouse gas emissions.

3. **Humanitarian Aid**:

- o **Disaster Response**: AI can help predict natural disasters like hurricanes or earthquakes and improve the efficiency of disaster relief efforts by analyzing satellite data and real-time reports.
- o **Poverty Alleviation**: AI is used to identify patterns in social and economic data, which can inform policies to help lift people out of poverty.

4. **Education**:

- o **Personalized Learning**: AI can tailor educational content to individual learning styles and needs, helping students learn more effectively.
- o **Automated Tutoring Systems**: AI-powered chatbots and tutoring systems can provide educational support to underserved communities where teachers are scarce.

AI for good not only benefits society but also fosters positive public perception of AI as a force for social change.

16.4 Ethical Frameworks: Overview of Ethical Guidelines and Frameworks for Responsible AI Development

As AI becomes more integrated into society, ethical considerations must guide its development and deployment. Several frameworks and guidelines have been proposed to ensure that AI is developed responsibly and benefits society.

Key Ethical Principles for AI:

1. **Fairness**: AI should be fair and not discriminate against any group based on race, gender, socioeconomic status, or other factors. Models should be tested and validated to ensure they are free from bias.

2. **Accountability**: Developers and organizations should be accountable for the decisions made by AI systems. Clear guidelines should be in place for addressing mistakes or harms caused by AI.

3. **Transparency**: AI systems should be transparent, with clear explanations of how decisions are made and how models function.

4. **Privacy**: AI should respect user privacy and comply with data protection regulations. Sensitive personal data should be handled securely and ethically.

5. **Safety and Security**: AI systems should be safe and secure, with robust mechanisms in place to prevent misuse or exploitation.

6. **Inclusivity**: AI should be designed to benefit all segments of society, particularly marginalized and vulnerable groups.

Ethical Frameworks for Responsible AI Development:

1. **The Asilomar AI Principles**:
   o A set of 23 guidelines developed by AI researchers, focusing on issues such as value alignment, safety, and privacy in AI systems.

2. **The EU AI Ethics Guidelines**:
   o Developed by the European Commission's High-Level Expert Group on AI, these guidelines emphasize trustworthiness in AI and provide specific principles for ethical AI development.

3. **The IEEE Global Initiative on Ethics of Autonomous and Intelligent Systems**:
   o Provides guidelines for designing and deploying AI and autonomous systems that are aligned with human well-being and rights.

223

4. **AI Now Institute Guidelines**:
   - Focuses on the social implications of AI and the need for transparency, accountability, and fairness in AI systems, especially regarding labor, privacy, and surveillance.

By following these ethical frameworks and principles, AI developers can ensure that their systems are not only technically effective but also socially responsible.

Summary

In this chapter, we:

- Explored **AI bias**, understanding how biases in data can lead to unfair and discriminatory outcomes, and discussed strategies for mitigating these biases.
- Learned the importance of **transparency and explainability** in AI systems, and how to make models more interpretable through techniques like **LIME** and **SHAP**.
- Delved into **AI for Good**, highlighting how AI can be used to solve social and global challenges, from healthcare to climate change.

- Reviewed key **ethical frameworks** and principles for responsible AI development, emphasizing fairness, accountability, transparency, and privacy.

Ethics in AI is an ongoing concern, and as the technology evolves, so too must the frameworks that govern its use. In the next chapter, we will explore the future of AI, discussing emerging technologies and their potential impact on society.

CHAPTER 17

BUILDING AN AI-POWERED CHATBOT

Chatbots have become an essential part of modern customer service, sales, and user engagement. They use AI to simulate human-like conversations, allowing businesses to interact with users automatically. Whether rule-based or powered by machine learning, chatbots can automate tasks, answer frequently asked questions, and improve overall user experience.

In this chapter, we will explore the process of building an AI-powered chatbot. We will cover **rule-based chatbots** (which rely on predefined rules) and **AI chatbots** (which use natural language processing (NLP) and machine learning techniques to understand and respond to user input). We will also discuss how to **deploy** your chatbot to popular messaging platforms like **Facebook Messenger** or **Slack**.

17.1 What is a Chatbot? Introduction to Chatbots and Their Applications

A **chatbot** is a software application designed to simulate human conversation. By using text or voice inputs, chatbots interact with users and provide responses in a conversational manner. Chatbots can be classified into two main categories:

1. **Rule-Based Chatbots**:
   o These chatbots operate based on predefined rules and patterns. They typically follow a decision tree structure, where specific user inputs are mapped to specific responses.
   o **Limitations**: They struggle with understanding complex or unstructured queries.
   o **Use Cases**: Simple tasks like answering frequently asked questions (FAQs), booking appointments, or providing basic information.

2. **AI Chatbots**:
   o These chatbots are powered by **Natural Language Processing (NLP)** and **machine learning** techniques, allowing them to

understand and generate human-like responses.

- o **Benefits**: They can handle more complex conversations, adapt to user input, and learn from interactions.
- o **Use Cases**: Customer support, personal assistants, and conversational AI for sales or marketing.

Popular Applications of Chatbots:

- **Customer Support**: Automating common customer service queries, reducing response times, and improving efficiency.
- **E-commerce**: Helping customers find products, answer questions, and process orders.
- **Healthcare**: Assisting with appointment bookings, health monitoring, and providing information on medical conditions.
- **Entertainment**: Engaging users with interactive content, quizzes, or games.

17.2 Building a Rule-Based Chatbot: Creating a Chatbot Using If-Else Rules and Patterns

Rule-based chatbots are simple to implement, as they work by defining a set of rules for user inputs and mapping them to specific responses. They typically rely on pattern matching techniques (such as keywords or phrases) to determine the appropriate action.

Steps to Build a Simple Rule-Based Chatbot:

1. **Define the Rules**: Identify a set of keywords or phrases that the chatbot will recognize. For each recognized input, define a corresponding response.
2. **Pattern Matching**: Match user input with predefined patterns or keywords using **if-else** statements.
3. **Responding to Users**: When a pattern is matched, the chatbot replies with a predefined response.

Example of a Simple Rule-Based Chatbot in Python:

python

```
def chatbot_response(user_input):
    # Define simple rules
    if 'hello' in user_input.lower():
```

```
        return "Hi there! How can I assist you
today?"
    elif 'bye' in user_input.lower():
        return "Goodbye! Have a great day!"
    elif 'order' in user_input.lower():
        return "Sure! What would you like to
order?"
    else:
        return "I'm sorry, I don't understand
that. Can you please rephrase?"


# Example interaction with the user
while True:
    user_input = input("You: ")
    if 'bye' in user_input.lower():
        print("Bot:",
chatbot_response(user_input))
        break
    else:
        print("Bot:",
chatbot_response(user_input))
```

In this simple chatbot:

- The bot responds to greetings, orders, and farewells using if-else statements.
- This is a very basic example, but it shows how rule-based chatbots work by matching specific patterns in user input.

Limitations of Rule-Based Chatbots:

- Limited ability to handle unexpected or complex queries.
- Responses are pre-programmed and cannot evolve over time.

17.3 Building an AI Chatbot: Using NLP Techniques and Machine Learning to Build a Chatbot That Can Understand and Respond to User Input

AI chatbots use advanced NLP and machine learning techniques to understand and process natural language input. These chatbots can handle a wide range of user queries and respond intelligently.

Steps to Build an AI Chatbot:

1. **Data Collection**: Collect conversation data (such as chat logs) to train the model.
2. **Preprocessing**: Clean and preprocess the text data (e.g., tokenization, removing stop words, lemmatization).
3. **Intent Detection**: Use NLP techniques to identify the user's intent (i.e., what the user wants to achieve).

231

4. **Response Generation**: Use a model to generate responses based on the user's query and the detected intent.

Example: Building an AI Chatbot Using a Pre-trained Model (e.g., GPT-3 or BERT):

For this example, we will use the **Hugging Face Transformers** library, which provides pre-trained models like **GPT-3** and **BERT** that can be fine-tuned for chatbot applications.

```python
from transformers import pipeline

# Load pre-trained model for conversational AI
chatbot = pipeline("conversational", model="microsoft/DialoGPT-medium")

# Example conversation
while True:
    user_input = input("You: ")
    if 'bye' in user_input.lower():
        print("Bot: Goodbye!")
        break
    else:
        response = chatbot(user_input)
```

```
    print("Bot:",
response[0]['generated_text'])
```

In this example:

- We use **DialoGPT**, a fine-tuned version of GPT-2 optimized for conversational responses.
- The chatbot generates contextually relevant replies to user input, making the conversation flow more naturally compared to rule-based systems.

Advantages of AI Chatbots:

- **Understanding Context**: AI chatbots can remember previous interactions and adjust their responses accordingly.
- **Adaptability**: They can improve over time by learning from new conversations.
- **Handling Complex Queries**: AI chatbots can process complex and open-ended queries, providing intelligent responses.

Challenges of AI Chatbots:

- **Training Data**: Requires a large corpus of conversational data to train the model effectively.

- **Resource-Intensive**: AI chatbots can require significant computational resources, especially for training deep learning models.

17.4 Deploying Your Chatbot: How to Deploy Your Chatbot to Messaging Platforms Like Facebook Messenger or Slack

Once your chatbot is developed, the next step is deployment. Deploying a chatbot involves integrating it into a platform where users can interact with it. Many platforms, such as **Facebook Messenger** and **Slack**, provide APIs for easily integrating bots.

Steps to Deploy a Chatbot:

1. **Choose a Platform**: Decide where your chatbot will be deployed (e.g., website, Slack, Facebook Messenger, WhatsApp).
2. **Create an API**: If using a machine learning-based chatbot, you may want to expose your model via a RESTful API using frameworks like **Flask** or **FastAPI**.

3. **Integrate with Messaging Platform**: Use the platform's API to connect your chatbot to the messaging service.

Example: Deploying a Chatbot on Facebook Messenger:

1. **Create a Facebook App**: Go to the **Facebook Developer Portal** and create a new app.
2. **Set Up Webhook**: A webhook is needed to handle incoming messages from users on Messenger. You can use **Flask** to set up a simple webhook.

python

```python
from flask import Flask, request, jsonify
import requests

app = Flask(__name__)

VERIFY_TOKEN = "your_verification_token"
PAGE_ACCESS_TOKEN = "your_page_access_token"

@app.route('/webhook', methods=['GET'])
def verify_webhook():
    # Verification request to ensure the webhook is legitimate
    if request.args.get("hub.verify_token") == VERIFY_TOKEN:
```

235

```python
        return request.args.get("hub.challenge")
    return 'Error, wrong verification token'

@app.route('/webhook', methods=['POST'])
def handle_message():
    # Handling the incoming message
    data = request.get_json()
    for entry in data['entry']:
        for message in entry['messaging']:
            text = message['message']['text']
            user_id = message['sender']['id']
            send_message(user_id, "You said: " +
text)
    return "OK", 200

def send_message(user_id, text):
    url                            =
f"https://graph.facebook.com/v10.0/me/messages?
access_token={PAGE_ACCESS_TOKEN}"
    message_data = {
        'recipient': {'id': user_id},
        'message': {'text': text}
    }
    response        =        requests.post(url,
json=message_data)
    return response

if __name__ == '__main__':
    app.run(debug=True, port=5000)
```

3. **Set Up Webhook URL in Facebook App**: Provide the URL of your deployed Flask app (e.g., using **Heroku** or **AWS**).

4. **Test the Chatbot**: Send messages to your Facebook Messenger bot and see how it responds.

Deploying on Slack:

1. **Create a Slack App**: Go to the **Slack API** page and create a new app.

2. **Set Up Event Subscriptions**: Set up event subscriptions to listen to incoming messages and interact with Slack's message API.

3. **Use Slack's SDK**: You can use **Slack Bolt** or **Slack SDK** to simplify the process of handling events and messages.

Summary

In this chapter, we:

- Explored the fundamentals of **chatbots**, their types, and real-world applications.

- Built a **rule-based chatbot** using simple pattern matching and if-else statements.

- Developed an **AI-powered chatbot** using **NLP** and **pre-trained models** like **DialoGPT**, allowing for more complex, human-like interactions.

- Learned how to **deploy** the chatbot to messaging platforms like **Facebook Messenger** and **Slack**, making the bot accessible to users in real-world environments.

Chatbots are revolutionizing customer service, entertainment, and business, and their ability to simulate human-like conversation makes them valuable tools across industries. In the next chapter, we will explore **advanced chatbot techniques**, such as multi-turn conversations and integrating with external APIs.

CHAPTER 18

AI IN THE REAL WORLD: CASE STUDIES

Artificial Intelligence (AI) is transforming industries worldwide by automating tasks, enhancing decision-making, and unlocking new possibilities. In this chapter, we will explore how AI is applied across different sectors, focusing on **healthcare**, **finance**, and **marketing**. We'll also analyze real-world case studies to highlight successful AI applications and the tangible impact they have had on businesses and society.

18.1 AI in Healthcare: How AI is Transforming the Healthcare Industry with Diagnostic Tools, Drug Discovery, and Patient Care

AI has made a significant impact in healthcare, revolutionizing the way medical professionals diagnose diseases, develop treatments, and manage patient care. AI-powered tools can analyze large datasets faster and more accurately than humans, making healthcare more efficient and accessible.

1. **Diagnostic Tools**:
   - **Medical Imaging**: AI models, particularly deep learning algorithms, are used to analyze medical images such as X-rays, MRIs, and CT scans to detect abnormalities. AI can identify patterns in the images that may not be visible to the human eye, enabling earlier detection of diseases like cancer.
     - **Case Study**: Google Health developed an AI model to detect breast cancer from mammograms with **higher accuracy** than radiologists. The AI system was trained on a large dataset of mammograms and was shown to outperform human doctors in some areas.

2. **Drug Discovery**:
   - AI is used to accelerate the process of drug discovery by analyzing vast amounts of

240

biological data. Machine learning models can predict the efficacy of drug compounds, reducing the time it takes to develop new treatments.

- **Case Study**: **Atomwise** uses AI to predict which drug compounds could be effective against diseases like Ebola and COVID-19. Their AI platform has helped identify promising compounds much faster than traditional methods.

3. **Personalized Medicine**:

   o AI is increasingly used in **personalized medicine**, where treatments are tailored to individual patients based on their genetic makeup, lifestyle, and other factors. AI models analyze patient data to recommend personalized treatment plans.

   - **Case Study**: **IBM Watson Health** uses AI to analyze medical literature and patient data to suggest personalized treatment options for cancer patients. The system has been used in several hospitals to assist doctors in making treatment decisions.

4. **Predictive Analytics**:

   o AI algorithms are used to predict the likelihood of patients developing certain conditions, such as diabetes or heart disease, based on historical data. This allows healthcare providers to take preventative actions before conditions become serious.

      ▪ **Case Study**: **DeepMind** collaborated with the NHS to create an AI system that can predict patient deterioration in real-time, enabling healthcare providers to intervene early and save lives.

Benefits of AI in Healthcare:

- Faster and more accurate diagnostics.
- Reduced healthcare costs by automating routine tasks.
- Improved treatment outcomes through personalized care.

Challenges:

- Ensuring data privacy and security, especially in medical applications.
- Overcoming regulatory hurdles in different countries.

18.2 AI in Finance: Using AI for Fraud Detection, Stock Market Predictions, and Customer Service

The finance industry has been quick to adopt AI for its ability to analyze large volumes of data and detect patterns that humans may miss. From improving fraud detection systems to enhancing customer service, AI is playing a crucial role in financial institutions.

Applications of AI in Finance:

1. **Fraud Detection**:
   o AI models are used to detect fraudulent transactions by analyzing transaction data in real-time. Machine learning algorithms learn from historical transaction patterns to identify anomalies that may indicate fraud.

243

- **Case Study**: **Mastercard** uses AI to detect fraudulent transactions by analyzing patterns of card usage. Their AI-powered system can identify suspicious behavior and block fraudulent transactions in real-time, reducing the risk of fraud for customers.

2. **Stock Market Predictions**:

   o AI and machine learning algorithms are widely used in stock market predictions, where they analyze historical market data to predict future trends. These models can process vast amounts of data from different sources, including social media, news, and financial reports.

     - **Case Study**: **QuantConnect** is a platform that provides AI-powered tools for quantitative finance. They use machine learning models to backtest trading strategies and predict stock prices, helping investors make informed decisions.

3. **Customer Service**:

- o AI-powered chatbots and virtual assistants are used by financial institutions to provide 24/7 customer service. These AI tools can handle a wide range of customer queries, from account balance inquiries to transaction processing.

  - **Case Study**: **Bank of America** has developed an AI-powered chatbot named **Erica**. Erica helps customers with tasks such as checking balances, making payments, and even providing financial advice based on customer behavior.

Benefits of AI in Finance:

- Improved efficiency in detecting and preventing fraud.
- Enhanced customer experiences through personalized financial services.
- Better decision-making in trading and investment.

Challenges:

- Ensuring that AI algorithms are not biased and that they operate fairly.

- Addressing concerns around job displacement in the financial industry.

18.3 AI in Marketing: Personalizing User Experiences and Optimizing Advertising Campaigns Using AI

AI has transformed marketing by allowing companies to personalize user experiences, optimize advertising campaigns, and predict customer behavior. AI-driven insights help marketers target the right audience with the right message at the right time.

Applications of AI in Marketing:

1. **Personalized Recommendations**:
   o AI is used to analyze user behavior and recommend products or services that are most likely to interest a customer. Personalized recommendations increase customer engagement and conversion rates.
     ▪ **Case Study**: **Amazon** uses AI to recommend products based on users' browsing and purchase history. Their recommendation engine drives a

significant portion of sales, with personalized suggestions accounting for over 35% of their revenue.

2. **Targeted Advertising**:

   o AI models analyze user data (e.g., browsing history, demographics, social media activity) to create highly targeted advertising campaigns. These campaigns deliver relevant ads to the right audience, increasing the effectiveness of advertising spend.

   - **Case Study**: **Facebook** uses AI to optimize advertising campaigns on its platform. By analyzing user interactions and behaviors, Facebook's AI system serves highly personalized ads, improving engagement and return on investment for advertisers.

3. **Customer Sentiment Analysis**:

   o AI can analyze social media, reviews, and customer feedback to gauge public sentiment about a brand, product, or service. This allows marketers to respond to customer

247

concerns in real-time and adjust their strategies accordingly.

- **Case Study**: **Coca-Cola** uses AI-powered sentiment analysis to monitor customer feedback across social media platforms. By analyzing positive and negative sentiment, Coca-Cola can quickly adapt its marketing campaigns and improve customer satisfaction.

4. **Chatbots and Virtual Assistants**:

   o AI-powered chatbots and virtual assistants are widely used in marketing to provide real-time customer support and guide customers through sales funnels.

   - **Case Study**: **Sephora**, a cosmetics brand, uses an AI-powered chatbot on its website and mobile app to help customers find products based on their preferences and previous purchases. The chatbot also provides personalized beauty advice, enhancing the customer experience.

Benefits of AI in Marketing:

- More personalized and relevant customer interactions.
- Optimized advertising spend by targeting the right audience.
- Real-time insights into customer behavior and market trends.

Challenges:

- Privacy concerns related to the use of personal data for targeted marketing.
- Balancing personalization with the need to avoid over-targeting and being perceived as invasive.

18.4 Case Study Analysis: Real-World Examples of Successful AI Applications

Let's take a closer look at some real-world case studies that demonstrate the transformative impact of AI across industries.

1. AI in Healthcare: PathAI

- **Company**: PathAI
- **Application**: PathAI uses machine learning models to assist pathologists in diagnosing diseases such as cancer. Their AI platform analyzes medical images (e.g., biopsies) to identify patterns that may indicate cancerous cells. This system improves diagnostic accuracy and speeds up the process, leading to better patient outcomes.
- **Outcome**: PathAI's technology has been proven to increase the accuracy of disease diagnoses, providing a valuable tool for healthcare professionals.

2. AI in Finance: JPMorgan's COiN

- **Company**: JPMorgan Chase
- **Application**: JPMorgan developed the **COiN** (Contract Intelligence) platform, an AI-powered tool that analyzes legal documents and extracts important data. This system automates the process of reviewing contracts, which traditionally took lawyers hours or even days to complete.
- **Outcome**: COiN has significantly reduced the time and cost associated with document review, enabling

JPMorgan to process thousands of contracts more efficiently.

3. AI in Marketing: Netflix

- **Company**: Netflix
- **Application**: Netflix uses AI for its recommendation engine, which suggests TV shows and movies to users based on their viewing history and preferences. This personalization helps improve user engagement and keeps subscribers loyal to the platform.
- **Outcome**: The recommendation system accounts for more than **80%** of the content viewed on Netflix, driving customer satisfaction and retention.

4. AI in Retail: Zara's AI-Powered Inventory Management

- **Company**: Zara (Inditex)
- **Application**: Zara uses AI to manage inventory and forecast demand for clothing items in its stores. By analyzing sales data, social media trends, and customer behavior, Zara's AI system ensures that the right products are stocked in the right quantities at the right time.
- **Outcome**: Zara's AI-driven inventory management system has enabled the company to reduce waste,

improve stock turnover, and increase overall efficiency in its retail operations.

Summary

In this chapter, we:

- Explored how **AI is transforming industries** like **healthcare**, **finance**, and **marketing** with practical applications such as diagnostic tools, fraud detection, and personalized recommendations.
- Analyzed real-world **case studies** from companies like **Google Health**, **JPMorgan**, **Netflix**, and **Zara** to highlight successful AI applications and their tangible impacts.
- Discussed both the **benefits** and **challenges** of integrating AI into business operations, from improving efficiency and accuracy to addressing ethical concerns related to data privacy and bias.

AI is revolutionizing industries by automating complex tasks, enabling smarter decision-making, and improving user experiences. As AI continues to evolve, its applications will expand even further, offering new opportunities for innovation. In the next chapter, we will explore the **future of AI**, focusing on emerging trends and technologies shaping the next generation of AI systems.

CHAPTER 19

DEBUGGING AND IMPROVING AI MODELS

Building an AI model is only half the battle. Once you have developed a model, it's essential to ensure that it performs well and is robust enough to handle real-world data. Debugging and improving the performance of AI models requires a systematic approach to identify issues such as overfitting, underfitting, poor data handling, and inefficient learning. In this chapter, we will cover the common pitfalls AI developers face, methods for debugging machine learning (ML) and deep learning (DL) models, and strategies for improving model accuracy.

19.1 Common AI Pitfalls: How to Avoid Overfitting, Underfitting, and Poor Data Handling

When developing AI models, there are several common pitfalls that can degrade model performance. Addressing these issues early in the development process can prevent suboptimal results.

1. Overfitting

Overfitting occurs when a model learns not only the underlying patterns in the training data but also the noise and random fluctuations, which do not generalize well to unseen data. In essence, the model becomes too complex, capturing too many details that don't apply to real-world data.

- **Signs of Overfitting**: If the model performs very well on the training data but poorly on the validation or test data, it's a sign that the model is overfitting.
- **Causes of Overfitting**:
  - Complex models with too many parameters.
  - Insufficient training data.
  - Lack of regularization.
- **How to Prevent Overfitting**:
  - **Cross-validation**: Use cross-validation to ensure the model generalizes well across different subsets of data.
  - **Regularization**: Techniques like **L2 regularization** (Ridge regression) or

dropout in deep learning prevent the model from becoming too complex.

o **Early Stopping**: Stop training the model when its performance on the validation set begins to degrade, even if performance on the training set continues to improve.

o **Reduce Model Complexity**: Use simpler models or reduce the number of parameters in complex models.

o **Increase Training Data**: More data helps the model generalize better and avoid memorizing the training set.

2. Underfitting

Underfitting occurs when a model is too simple to capture the underlying patterns in the data. The model fails to learn even the basic relationships in the dataset, leading to poor performance on both the training and test sets.

- **Signs of Underfitting**: If the model performs poorly on both training and test data, it's likely underfitting.
- **Causes of Underfitting**:

- o Model is too simple (e.g., using a linear model for data that has complex non-linear relationships).
- o Insufficient training or inadequate feature selection.

- **How to Prevent Underfitting**:
  - o **Increase Model Complexity**: Use more complex models like deep neural networks for non-linear data.
  - o **Feature Engineering**: Add more meaningful features or transform existing features to help the model capture more patterns in the data.
  - o **Increase Training Time**: Allow the model to train for longer periods to learn more patterns from the data.

3. Poor Data Handling

AI models are heavily reliant on high-quality data. Issues like poor data quality, incorrect preprocessing, and insufficient data can lead to inaccurate models.

- **Signs of Poor Data Handling**: If the model fails to learn or performs erratically, it may indicate issues with the data quality.

257

- **Common Data Handling Issues**:
  - o **Missing Data**: Missing values can result in biased or incorrect predictions if not handled properly.
  - o **Noisy Data**: Outliers or errors in the data can affect model training.
  - o **Imbalanced Data**: If certain classes are overrepresented or underrepresented in the training data, the model might be biased toward the majority class.
- **How to Handle Poor Data**:
  - o **Data Cleaning**: Handle missing values by imputation or deletion. Remove outliers that may distort model training.
  - o **Resampling**: For imbalanced datasets, use techniques like **SMOTE (Synthetic Minority Over-sampling Technique)** to balance the classes.
  - o **Data Augmentation**: In the case of image data, augmenting the dataset by applying transformations like rotations, flips, and zoom can increase the diversity of the data and prevent overfitting.

19.2 Debugging Techniques: Tools and Methods for Debugging Machine Learning and Deep Learning Models

Debugging machine learning and deep learning models can be more challenging than traditional software debugging due to the black-box nature of AI models. However, there are several methods and tools available to help identify and resolve issues.

1. Debugging Model Behavior with Evaluation Metrics

Use various evaluation metrics to understand the behavior of your model:

- **Confusion Matrix**: Helps identify whether the model is confusing certain classes (e.g., false positives and false negatives).
- **Precision, Recall, and F1-Score**: Evaluate how well the model is performing on specific classes, especially in imbalanced datasets.
- **Learning Curves**: Plotting training and validation error over time helps identify whether the model is overfitting or underfitting.

python

```
from  sklearn.metrics   import  confusion_matrix,
classification_report
import seaborn as sns
import matplotlib.pyplot as plt

# Generate confusion matrix
cm = confusion_matrix(y_test, y_pred)
sns.heatmap(cm, annot=True, fmt='d')
plt.show()

# Generate classification report
print(classification_report(y_test, y_pred))
```

2. Visualizing Model Predictions

Visualization tools can help debug deep learning models by showing which features are being used by the model for its predictions. For instance, with **convolutional neural networks (CNNs)**, you can visualize the activations of different layers to understand how the model is processing the data.

- **Saliency Maps**: Highlight the parts of an image that contribute most to the model's decision.
- **Grad-CAM**: Visualizes the areas of an image that are most influential in the model's prediction.

```
python
```

```
import cv2
import numpy as np
import matplotlib.pyplot as plt
from keras.preprocessing import image
from keras.applications.vgg16 import VGG16,
preprocess_input

# Load a pre-trained model
model = VGG16(weights='imagenet')

# Load an image
img            =            image.load_img('image.jpg',
target_size=(224, 224))
img_array = image.img_to_array(img)
img_array = np.expand_dims(img_array, axis=0)
img_array = preprocess_input(img_array)

# Get the model's predictions
predictions = model.predict(img_array)

# Generate Grad-CAM visualization (example for
VGG16)
# (Further implementation of Grad-CAM is required
here)
```

3. Hyperparameter Tuning and Grid Search

Sometimes, models need to be tuned for optimal performance. **Grid search** and **random search** are techniques for tuning hyperparameters (e.g., learning rate, batch size, number of hidden layers) to improve model accuracy.

python

```
from sklearn.model_selection import GridSearchCV
from            sklearn.ensemble           import
RandomForestClassifier

# Define parameter grid
param_grid = {'n_estimators': [50, 100, 200],
'max_depth': [10, 20, None]}

# Initialize model and grid search
grid_search                                       =
GridSearchCV(estimator=RandomForestClassifier()
, param_grid=param_grid, cv=5)
grid_search.fit(X_train, y_train)

# Print best hyperparameters
print(f"Best                     Parameters:
{grid_search.best_params_}")
```

4. Debugging Deep Learning Models with TensorFlow or PyTorch

Both **TensorFlow** and **PyTorch** provide debugging tools like `TensorBoard` and `Torch.utils.tensorboard` that allow you to visualize the training process, monitor gradients, and track performance over time.

```python
# In TensorFlow, use TensorBoard to monitor the
training process
from tensorflow.keras.callbacks import
TensorBoard

tensorboard = TensorBoard(log_dir='./logs')
model.fit(X_train, y_train, epochs=10,
callbacks=[tensorboard])
```

19.3 Improving Model Performance: Techniques to Improve the Accuracy of Your Models, Including Data Augmentation and Feature Engineering

Improving model performance requires a combination of better data, improved model architecture, and fine-tuning. Here are some techniques to enhance the accuracy of your AI models:

1. Data Augmentation

Data augmentation is particularly useful in domains like image classification. It involves artificially increasing the size of the dataset by applying random transformations to the original data (e.g., rotation, flipping, cropping, zooming).

```python

from keras.preprocessing.image import ImageDataGenerator

# Create an ImageDataGenerator instance
datagen = ImageDataGenerator(rotation_range=40,
width_shift_range=0.2, height_shift_range=0.2,
shear_range=0.2, zoom_range=0.2,
horizontal_flip=True)

# Apply transformations to training data
datagen.fit(X_train)
```

2. Feature Engineering

Feature engineering involves creating new features or transforming existing features to improve model performance. This can include:

- **Normalization/Standardization**: Scaling data so that it has zero mean and unit variance.
- **Polynomial Features**: Generating higher-order features for linear models.
- **Encoding Categorical Variables**: Using techniques like **one-hot encoding** or **label encoding** to handle categorical data.

264

3. Model Ensemble Techniques

Ensemble methods combine multiple models to improve prediction accuracy. Common ensemble techniques include:

- **Bagging**: Combining multiple models of the same type to improve stability (e.g., **Random Forest**).
- **Boosting**: Iteratively improving weak models by focusing on the mistakes made by previous models (e.g., **XGBoost**, **AdaBoost**).
- **Stacking**: Combining predictions from multiple different models.

4. Model Architecture Improvements

For deep learning models, exploring different architectures (e.g., changing the number of layers, using dropout layers, etc.) and regularization techniques can often lead to improved performance.

Summary

In this chapter, we:

- Examined common AI pitfalls such as **overfitting**, **underfitting**, and **poor data handling**, and discussed strategies to avoid them.
- Learned about debugging techniques, including the use of **evaluation metrics**, **visualizations**, and **hyperparameter tuning** to identify and fix issues in AI models.
- Explored methods for improving model performance, including **data augmentation**, **feature engineering**, and **ensemble techniques**.

Debugging and improving AI models is an iterative process that requires constant attention and fine-tuning. In the next chapter, we will discuss **AI model deployment**, focusing on how to deploy AI models into production and integrate them into real-world applications.

CHAPTER 20

FINAL PROJECT: BUILDING YOUR FIRST AI APPLICATION

In the final chapter of this book, we will put everything you've learned into practice by building a complete AI application. This project will bring together all the concepts and techniques you've studied, from data preprocessing to building AI models and deploying them. By the end of this chapter, you will have built a fully functional AI application.

The project we'll build is an **AI Personal Assistant** that can perform tasks such as setting reminders, fetching weather data, and managing a to-do list. This AI assistant will integrate various aspects of AI, including natural language processing (NLP), web scraping, and task automation.

20.1 Bringing It All Together: A Hands-On, Step-by-Step Guide to Building a Complete AI Application Using Everything You've Learned in the Book

Building an AI-powered personal assistant requires integrating various components, such as **speech recognition**, **natural language processing (NLP)**, **web scraping**, and **task automation**. We will break down the process into manageable steps.

Step 1: Set Up the Development Environment

Before diving into the code, ensure that your development environment is ready. We will need the following libraries and tools:

- **Python 3.x**: The core programming language for this project.
- **Speech Recognition**: For voice input capabilities.
- **NLP Libraries**: For processing natural language (e.g., **spaCy**, **NLTK**, or **transformers**).
- **Weather API**: To fetch weather data (we'll use **OpenWeatherMap API** for this).
- **Task Management**: To handle tasks like adding, removing, and listing to-do items.

- **Text-to-Speech (TTS)**: To respond to users in a conversational manner (we'll use **pyttsx3**).

Install the necessary Python libraries:

```bash

pip install speechrecognition pyttsx3 spacy
requests
```

Step 2: Define the Core Features of the AI Personal Assistant

Our AI assistant will have the following core features:

1. **Speech Recognition**: The assistant will listen to voice commands from the user.
2. **Weather Forecasting**: The assistant will fetch real-time weather data based on user requests.
3. **To-Do List Management**: The assistant will maintain and update a simple to-do list.
4. **Reminder Setting**: The assistant will set reminders for the user.

Step 3: Start with Speech Recognition and Text-to-Speech

First, we will integrate speech recognition to capture voice input and text-to-speech to provide verbal responses.

```python

import speech_recognition as sr
import pyttsx3

# Initialize the recognizer and the text-to-speech engine
recognizer = sr.Recognizer()
engine = pyttsx3.init()

def speak(text):
    """Convert text to speech."""
    engine.say(text)
    engine.runAndWait()

def listen():
    """Listen for user input using the microphone."""
    with sr.Microphone() as source:
        print("Listening for a command...")
        audio = recognizer.listen(source)
        try:
            query = recognizer.recognize_google(audio)
            print(f"You said: {query}")
            return query.lower()
        except sr.UnknownValueError:
            speak("Sorry, I did not understand that.")
```

```
        return None
    except sr.RequestError:
        speak("Sorry,    I'm   having   trouble
with the speech recognition service.")
        return None
```

Here, we set up the basic infrastructure for voice input and output. The `listen` function captures the user's voice input, and `speak` is used to provide audio feedback to the user.

Step 4: Implement Weather Fetching Functionality

We will fetch real-time weather data from an API. For this, we will use the **OpenWeatherMap API**. First, sign up for a free account on their website and get an API key.

python

```python
import requests

def get_weather(city):
    """Fetch     weather     information     from
OpenWeatherMap API."""
    api_key = "YOUR_API_KEY"  # Replace with your
OpenWeatherMap API key
    base_url                                    =
f"http://api.openweathermap.org/data/2.5/weathe
r?q={city}&appid={api_key}&units=metric"
```

```
try:
    response = requests.get(base_url)
    data = response.json()
    if data["cod"] == 200:
        main = data["main"]
        temperature = main["temp"]
        description                    =
data["weather"][0]["description"]
        return f"The current temperature in
{city} is {temperature}°C with {description}."
    else:
        return "Sorry, I couldn't retrieve
the weather data."
    except requests.exceptions.RequestException
as e:
        return f"An error occurred: {e}"
```

This function queries the **OpenWeatherMap API** and retrieves the current temperature and weather description for a given city.

Step 5: Create the To-Do List Functionality

We will implement a simple in-memory to-do list where the assistant can add, remove, and display tasks.

```python
python
```

```
to_do_list = []
```

```python
def add_task(task):
    """Add a task to the to-do list."""
    to_do_list.append(task)
    return f"Task '{task}' added to your to-do list."

def remove_task(task):
    """Remove a task from the to-do list."""
    if task in to_do_list:
        to_do_list.remove(task)
        return f"Task '{task}' removed from your to-do list."
    else:
        return f"Task '{task}' not found in your to-do list."

def show_tasks():
    """Show all tasks in the to-do list."""
    if to_do_list:
        return "Here are your tasks: " + ", ".join(to_do_list)
    else:
        return "Your to-do list is empty."
```

This code allows the assistant to manage a simple list of tasks. You can add tasks with the add_task function, remove them with remove_task, and display all tasks with show_tasks.

273

20.2 Project: AI Personal Assistant

Now that we have built the individual components, let's combine everything into a working AI personal assistant that can respond to voice commands.

python

```python
def main():
    """Main function to interact with the AI
personal assistant."""
    speak("Hello, I am your personal assistant.
How can I help you today?")

    while True:
        query = listen()

        if query is None:
            continue

        # Weather Query
        if "weather" in query:
            speak("Which city would you like to
know the weather for?")
            city = listen()
            if city:
                weather = get_weather(city)
```

```
        speak(weather)

    # To-Do List Management
    elif "add task" in query:
        speak("What task would you like to
add?")
        task = listen()
        if task:
            speak(add_task(task))

    elif "remove task" in query:
        speak("What task would you like to
remove?")
        task = listen()
        if task:
            speak(remove_task(task))

    elif "show tasks" in query:
        speak(show_tasks())

    # Exit Command
    elif "exit" in query or "bye" in query:
        speak("Goodbye! Have a great day!")
        break

if __name__ == "__main__":
    main()
```

In this final integration:

- The assistant listens to the user's voice command.
- It can check the weather, add/remove tasks, or show the to-do list based on the user's query.
- The assistant continues running until the user says "exit" or "bye".

20.3 Code Walkthrough and Best Practices: A Detailed Explanation of the Project's Code and Design

1. Code Structure and Design

- **Modularity**: The code is modularized, with separate functions for speech recognition, weather fetching, and task management. This makes the application maintainable and easy to extend with additional features.
- **Error Handling**: Error handling is implemented to manage issues like misrecognition of speech or failed API calls.
- **User Interaction**: The assistant provides feedback using both text-to-speech and written output, creating a seamless user experience.

276

2. Best Practices for Developing AI Applications

1. **Data Privacy**: Always ensure that user data is handled securely. If the application stores sensitive data, use proper encryption techniques and ensure compliance with privacy regulations.

2. **Model Evaluation**: For AI-powered applications, it's important to regularly evaluate the performance of the models, whether it's for NLP, recommendation, or predictive tasks.

3. **Scalability**: Ensure that the application can scale by using cloud services, especially when integrating with external APIs, like weather data fetching or task management.

4. **User Feedback**: Continuously collect and incorporate user feedback to improve the assistant's functionality, making it more intelligent and efficient over time.

5. **Error Logging**: Implement error logging for debugging and improving the application. This helps in tracking issues in a production environment.

Summary

In this chapter, we:

- Built an **AI Personal Assistant** that can perform tasks like setting reminders, fetching weather data, and managing a to-do list using **speech recognition**, **natural language processing (NLP)**, and **API integration**.
- Walked through the key components of the AI assistant, including the **speech-to-text, text-to-speech**, and **weather-fetching functions**.
- Explored best practices for developing and deploying AI applications, focusing on modularity, error handling, and scalability.

This final project demonstrates how AI can be applied to real-world tasks, providing a solid foundation for developing more complex AI-powered applications in the future.

CONCLUSION

Congratulations! You've now completed the journey of building and understanding AI applications from the ground up. Over the course of this book, we've explored the various aspects of Artificial Intelligence—covering foundational concepts, developing machine learning models, addressing real-world challenges, and deploying AI solutions. This final chapter has helped you bring everything together by building a practical AI application: an **AI-powered personal assistant**.

What We Learned:

- **AI Fundamentals**: We began by understanding the core concepts of AI, machine learning, and deep learning. We explored how these technologies are shaping industries and our daily lives.
- **Building AI Models**: We walked through the process of designing, training, and evaluating machine learning and deep learning models, learning how to overcome common pitfalls like overfitting and underfitting.

- **Real-World Applications**: We saw how AI is transforming sectors like healthcare, finance, marketing, and more, with real-world case studies showcasing AI's potential to solve critical problems.

- **Practical AI Development**: You gained hands-on experience building AI models and integrating them into applications, including creating a chatbot, building a recommendation system, and deploying your model to cloud platforms.

- **Ethics and Best Practices**: We discussed the ethical considerations in AI, emphasizing the importance of fairness, transparency, and accountability, which are essential for developing responsible AI systems.

- **Scaling and Deployment**: We delved into the technicalities of scaling AI projects, training models on large datasets, and deploying AI solutions to production environments.

Your Next Steps:

As you've seen, AI has the potential to revolutionize industries, automate processes, and enhance decision-making. Now that you have the skills to build AI models and applications, there are many opportunities for you to continue learning and expanding your knowledge:

- **Experiment with New Projects**: Challenge yourself by creating new AI applications. Whether it's a personal assistant, a recommendation engine, or an AI model for a specific problem, the possibilities are endless.

- **Contribute to Open-Source AI Projects**: Contributing to open-source AI projects can deepen your understanding of advanced techniques while helping you connect with a community of AI practitioners.

- **Stay Updated**: The field of AI is constantly evolving. Stay updated with the latest research papers, blog posts, and tutorials to keep refining your skills.

Final Thoughts:

The AI journey doesn't end here. Now that you have the foundational knowledge, you can dive deeper into specialized topics like reinforcement learning, computer vision, natural language processing, and more. AI is a powerful tool that is already reshaping the world, and with your new skills, you have the ability to be part of this transformation.

Keep experimenting, keep building, and most importantly, keep learning. The future of AI is full of opportunities, and you're well-equipped to take on the challenges and innovations that lie ahead.

Thank you for joining me on this AI journey. I hope this book has empowered you to build and deploy AI applications, and I wish you the best of luck in your future AI endeavors!

Printed in Dunstable, United Kingdom